COMMUNICATIONS

COMMUNICATIONS

by

Raymond Williams

Revised Edition

1966

CHATTO & WINDUS

London

Published by
Chatto & Windus Ltd
40 William IV Street
London W.C.2

*

Clarke, Irwin & Co. Limited
Toronto

First Published by
Penguin Books Limited, 1962
Revised Edition, 1966

CONTENTS

ACKNOWLEDGEMENTS

I wish to thank my wife for much detailed help with this book. I have also been helped by my daughter and my sons, in certain parts. I owe a good deal to my friends Graham Martin and Stuart Hall, with whom I have worked on and discussed some of these issues. I wish also to acknowledge the initiative of the National Union of Teachers, in calling the conference on 'Popular Culture and Personal Responsibility', which was the most remarkable event of its kind ever held in this country, and which greatly stimulated and helped me.

In preparing the revised edition, I was again greatly helped by my wife, and, on specific points, by Martin Bernal, Elias Bredsdorff, and members of the Modern Languages Faculty at Cambridge.

R.W.

Preface to the Second Edition

THIS book was first written as a Penguin Special, in the series 'Britain in the Sixties'. As such, it addressed itself to immediate problems of social and cultural policy, yet necessarily through description and analysis of the structure and content of our existing institutions and systems. This part of the work was based on methods and material I had been using in adult education classes, and it happened that just at the time I was writing it I was changing my job, from extra-mural to internal university teaching; I was gathering up what had been done there, and what might easily have been lost.

In its original form, the book sold out very quickly, and there has been a continuing demand for it, beyond the special context in which it was originally conceived. In particular there has been a demand for it in educational courses and syllabuses, where the issues it deals with are increasingly being studied. I have been down to my own last copy for some three or four years, and yet I was not sure, in my own very different teaching situation, that I could go back and revise it, so that it could be made available again. University teaching is extraordinarily stimulating, but it is remarkable how much it excludes: both in the simple sense of the syllabus, where this kind of work is only just beginning, in England, to enter the university field; and in the more complex sense, of the cultural atmosphere of a university, in which there are strong pressures to confine oneself to the traditional interests and habits of minority education, so that issues and institutions affecting majorities tend to fade. I became conscious of the full extent of this influence only when I came back to this work, and felt the weight and challenge of its pressures.

Other things have happened in the intervening years. I have been pleased to see how much I needed to add and revise, in my chapter on proposals, to take account of what is still slow but undoubtedly a change and a movement. It is easy to see, looking back, that from 1956 to 1962 there was an intense development of ideas in the field of culture and communications, and by the time of the Pilkington Report this had reached the level of open and conventional politics. This development has had two results. First, that a current of opinion, and the necessary work to support it, has been decisively introduced into social argument. The great merit of earlier work in this field, of the phase associated with 'Scrutiny', was its remarkable and still growing influence in education: critical work, on the content of popular culture, has now a long and still exciting history in many of our schools. The mark of the second phase, which is normally associated with the 'New Left', has been an extension to the problems of institutions: both their immediate amendment and reform, and the discovery of newly possible institutions for a democratic culture. There are still many tensions between the two phases: the arguments about a minority culture and a democratic culture often and necessarily divide them. But also, in actual work, there is important common ground, and their combined influence has had an evident public effect. We have developed in Britain, if still unevenly, as good a critical education, in these new fields, as exists anywhere. And it is equally important that, as was said recently, 'the original critique of the capitalist organization of culture has, uniquely in the advanced capitalist world, been given a precise programmatic edge'. These gains, marked by many local signs and by a visible alteration of the dimensions and terms of the argument, are naturally encouraging.

But it is then time to remember the second result. There was a point, quite evident to me between the publication of *The Long Revolution* and *Communications*, and evident in the most public way in reactions to the Pilkington Report, when a genuine and powerful counter-attack was mounted and developed. This expressed itself first in the form intrinsic to a fashionable culture: that these things had been said too often, and were becoming boring; it was time to move on, though it was never clear to what. A second kind of reaction, familiar in the long history of English attempts at change, was the absorption, containment and apparent neutralisation of the offending ideas: they came back to one, with echoes reminding one of their source, but subtly transformed and in effect integrated into a defence of existing institutions and practices, though with just a sufficient residue of manageable disquiet to interlock with feelings that might otherwise get out of hand. And then, of course, there was the direct and open attack, from the existing interests: the shocking misrepresentation of the Pilkington Report, by newspapers themselves involved in commercial television, is a study in itself.

And all the time, beyond this ebb and flow of opinion, the basic character of our major cultural institutions was not only unchanged, but was becoming more settled, more established, and more widely integrated with a whole variety of other activities. It was when I saw this, and when I fully realised the nature of the counter-attack (which, of course, as intended, had sapped one's energy, the more effectively because traditional and comfortable directions were readily and even pressingly open), that I knew I must do the necessary work to make this book available again. It was a book conceived on a small scale, for a particular purpose, and I still wish I had the resources to make it larger and better. I am particularly glad that work of a long-term kind is now going on, at the Centre for Contemporary Cultural Studies in Birmingham, under Richard Hoggart and Stuart Hall. Many of the details of my own work will, I hope, be superseded by longer and better equipped research. But there was still room, it seemed, for this kind of study, as an introduction and with a certain edge.

The revisions and additions I have made are mainly in the chapters on 'Content' and on 'Proposals'. I have added tables for 1965 to the original 1961 tables, for comparison and continuity. (It is worth briefly mentioning here the complementary work, following the same tables but on the Danish press, in the Danish edition of this book – *Massemedierne*, Copenhagen, 1963.) I have also included some new analysis, including comparisons of a limited kind with some foreign newspapers, and a different type of comparison of headlines. In the chapter on 'Proposals' I have been mainly concerned to keep up with a continuing argument. I have also added two appendices, on methods in television education, and on the valuable White Paper 'A Policy for the Arts'.

It remains to make two general points, which I place in this preface for emphasis. The first concerns my proposal that the right kind of organization, for any cultural institution, is one based on control by the contributors. This excited some interest but also some ribaldry: I was asked to imagine a *Daily Express* controlled by its contributors, and then say what gain there had been. In fact, of course, there would then be no *Daily Express* at all; it isn't that kind of organ. More serious doubts were also raised: whether there could ever be this kind of change, with the contributors as they were, and whether one had not really to think of wholesale change and replacement.

Now it is not that conflict can, by any means, be eliminated (some of it will be severe and will involve radical replacements), but the whole perspective of my work in this field has been based on a particular theory of the nature of change in this kind of society (its fullest statement is in the first chapters of *The Long Revolution*). Briefly, I do not believe we can go on posing a change of institutions and a change of attitudes as alternatives. From each polarity follows a rigid programme: in the first case, destruction and then innovation of institutions, imagined at some finite point in time; in the second case, a rejection of politics and social activity, with criticism becoming an activity in itself, refining attitudes and responses, but able to be an activity in itself only by an acceptance, however sullen, of all other existing social habits and structures. Each position shares a certain negative character: an intransigent group against the whole social structure; an intransigent group against the whole intellectual structure. As such, each corresponds to the positive needs of many intellectuals in our society; each attitude, I may say, forms almost every day in my own mind. Basically, they are the last, and of course serious, positions of our pre-democratic politics; change, there, is essentially against others; to change with others is seen as compromise. Each group, similarly, accepts the liberal separation between individuals and societies, and the related separation between cultural content and cultural institutions; the divergence comes only when one or other separate entity is seen as decisive.

My reply, then, to the point about the existing contributors and their institutions, which seem so often so well suited to each other, is that the observation is made in a wholly static and separatist way, with no real attention to the complex ways in which individuals are formed by the institutions to which they belong, and in which, by reaction, the institutions take on the colour of individuals thus formed. The changes I propose are in terms of growth: that we can find ways to intervene in this continuing process, by a realisation and assertion of our own shared needs, and that in the shock of this intervention there is a good chance of the changes of substance which I do not believe can come in any other way. The individuals and the institutions will have, essentially, to change together, or they will not change at all. And my reason for going on working on these lines is that I know, from observing myself and others, in very different institutions, that this is a continuing process, in which the moments of choice and of direction are often subtle and delicate, though the commitments they lead to are often profound. What I have tried to envisage is a radical change which yet includes a human continuity, and I believe the pressure for this, in our actual society, is the most intense and valuable pressure we have. The job of any of us working in this field is articulation, for it is when it is articulate that the pressure becomes a discipline and a programme.

What I have said about growth can be related to the idea of permanent education, which is now so important in French cultural thought, and with which I have had valuable recent contacts. This idea seems to me to repeat, in a new and important idiom, the concepts of learning and of popular democratic culture which underlie the present book. What it valuably stresses is the educational force (*éducation* as distinct from *enseignement*) of our whole social and cultural experience. It is therefore concerned, not only with continuing education, of a formal or informal kind, but with what the whole environment, its institutions and relationships, actively and profoundly teaches. To consider the problems of families, or of town planning, is then an educational enterprise, for these, also, are where teaching occurs. And then the field of this book, of the cultural communications which, under an old shadow, are still called mass communications, can be integrated, as I had always intended, with a whole social policy. For who can doubt, looking at television or newspapers, or reading the women's magazines, that here, centrally, is *teaching*, and teaching financed and distributed in a much larger way than is formal education?

The choice is then clear. The need for permanent education, in our kind of changing society, will be met in one way or another. It is now on the whole being met, though with many valuable exceptions and efforts against the tide, by an integration of this teaching with the priorities and interests of a capitalist society, and of a capitalist society, moreover, which necessarily retains as its central principle (though against powerful pressures, of a democratic kind, from the rest of our social experience) the idea of a few governing, communicating with and teaching the many. I have been deeply impressed, looking again at this material, by the extent to which it is in itself integrated. Organized economically, in its largest part, around advertising, it is increasingly organized culturally around the values and habits of that version of human personality, human need and human capacity. This strong and integrated world is capable, I believe, in the coming decades, of adapting to its own purposes both politics and education. In politics it has already made extraordinary advances, in the style of campaigns and in its projected versions of power. In education the pressures are already strong, and can foreseeably be strengthened by the wrong use of new media of teaching. And in education, ironically, the last-ditch stand of a minority culture can become a point of entry. A reserved area for an elite education (some of which is now in fact put directly to use in advertising and public relations) can be made the basis for limiting that genuinely popular education which the system has good reason to fear.

Against that kind of permanent education, already well organized and visibly extending its methods and its range, an integrated alternative is now profoundly necessary. I have seen something of the plans, in many countries, for a permanent education of a democratic and popular kind: programmes for family care, for the improvement and extension of schools, universities and further education, for the public safeguarding of natural beauty, for the planning of towns and cities around the needs of leisure and of learning, for the recovery of control and meaning in work. It is in the spirit of this kind of programme that I discuss communications, the field in which one or other version of a permanent education will be decisive. It is a particular field, and needs detailed and continuing study. But it is also the field in which our ideas of the world, of ourselves and of our possibilities, are most widely and often most powerfully formed and disseminated. To work for the recovery of control in this field is then, under any pressures, a priority.

I
Definitions

WHAT do we mean by communication? The oldest
meaning of the word, in English, can be summarized as
the passing of ideas, information, and attitudes from
person to person. But, later, communication came also
to mean a line or channel from place to place. Since the
Industrial Revolution there has been so much improvement in this kind of communication – in canals,
railways, steamships, cars, aircraft – that often, when
we say communications, we mean these ways of
travelling and carrying. Yet there is another major line
of modern improvement and invention. Steam printing, the electric telegraph, photography, wireless, film,
television are, like the computer with which, in a very
new way, the print of this book was composed, new
ways of passing ideas, information, and attitudes from
person to person, and we call them, also, communications. So that now the word has different meanings in
common use, and there is often confusion between
them. I think that for describing the physical means of
travelling and carrying, our other word, transport, is
better than communications, but I suppose both will go
on being used. In any case, in this book, I mean by
communications the institutions and forms in which
ideas, information, and attitudes are transmitted and
received. I mean by communication the process of
transmission and reception.

In our own generation, there has been a dramatic
tightening of interest in this world of communications.
The development of powerful new means of commun-

ication has coincided, historically, with the extension of democracy and with the attempts, by many kinds of ruling group, to control and manage democracy. The development has also coincided with important changes in the nature of work and in education, which have given many people new kinds of social opportunity. There has been a great expansion in the scale of ordinary society, both through the new communications systems and through the growth of many kinds of large-scale organization. Acting together, these developments have created social problems which seem to be of a quite new kind.

The growth of interest in communications is an important response to this new situation. It came, really, as a breakthrough in experience, cutting across our usual categories. Already some of our basic ideas of society are being changed by this new emphasis. From one familiar approach, through traditional politics, we have seen the central facts of society as power and government. From another familiar approach, through traditional economics, we have seen the central concerns of society as property, production, and trade. These approaches remain important, but they are now joined by a new emphasis: that society is a form of communication, through which experience is described, shared, modified, and preserved. We are used to descriptions of our whole common life in political and economic terms. The emphasis on communications asserts, as a matter of experience, that men and societies are not confined to relationships of power, property, and production. Their relationships in describing, learning, persuading, and exchanging experiences are seen as equally fundamental. This emphasis is exceptionally important in the long crisis of twentieth-century society. Many people, starting from older versions of society, have seen the growth of modern communications not as an expansion of men's powers to learn and to exchange ideas and experiences, but as a new method of government or a new opportunity for trade. All the new means of communication have been abused, for political control (as in propaganda) or for commercial profit (as in advertising). We can protest against such uses, but unless we have a clear alternative version of human society we are not likely to make our protests effective.

My own view is that we have been wrong in taking communication as secondary. Many people seem to assume as a matter of course that there is, first, reality, and then, second, communication about it. We degrade art and learning by supposing that they are always second-hand activities: that there is life, and then afterwards there are these accounts of it. Our commonest political error is the assumption that power – the capacity to govern other men – is the reality of the whole social process, and so the only context of politics. Our commonest economic error is the assumption that production and trade are our only practical activities, and that they require no other human justification or scrutiny. We need to say what many of us know in experience: that the life of man, and the business of society, cannot be confined to these ends; that the struggle to learn, to describe, to understand, to educate, is a central and necessary part of our humanity. This struggle is not begun, at second hand, after reality has occurred. It is, in itself, a major way in which reality is continually formed and changed. What we call society is not only a network of political and economic arrangements, but also a process of learning and communication.

Communication begins in the struggle to learn and to

describe. To start this process in our minds, and to pass on its results to others, we depend on certain communication models, certain rules or conventions through which we can make contact. We can change these models, when they become inadequate, or we can modify and extend them. Our efforts to do so, and to use the existing models successfully, take up a large part of our living energy. The history of a language is a record of efforts of this kind, and is as central a part of the history of a people as its changing political and economic institutions. Moreover, many of our communication models become, in themselves, social institutions. Certain attitudes to others, certain forms of address, certain tones and styles, become embodied in institutions which are then very powerful in social effect. The crisis in modern communications has been caused by the speed of invention and by the difficulty of finding the right institutions in which these technical means are to be used. In modern Britain, we have a whole range of uses of printing, of photography, of television, which do not necessarily follow from the technical means themselves. Many have been shaped by changing political and economic forces. Many, also, have been shaped by what are really particular communication models: the idea that speaking or writing to many people at once is speaking or writing to 'the masses'; the idea that there are clear types of people and interest – 'Third Programme', 'Home Service', and 'Light'; 'quality' and 'popular' – that we can separate and label. These arguable assumptions are often embodied in solid practical institutions, which then teach the models from which they start. We cannot examine the process of general communication in modern society without examining the shapes of these institutions. Further, if we understand the importance of communication, in all our social activities, we find that in examining the process and the institutions we are also looking at our society – at some of our characteristic relationships – in new ways.

This book is an introduction to this field of inquiry. It begins with an outline of the history of our modern means and institutions of communication. It goes on to examine, in various ways, some of the methods and content of some of our most important institutions. It then passes to the very lively arguments and controversies which have sprung up around these institutions, and which seem to be extending and intensifying year by year, as the sense of crisis mounts. It turns finally to a series of suggestions and proposals, which can be used as a basis for a general discussion of possible developments and changes.

I have been working in this field now for many years, and I am very conscious of the difficulties involved in any short book on so complicated and controversial a subject. So far as possible, I have based the book on methods of teaching which I have used over several years in classes for members of the Workers' Education Association and for trade unionists. The object, in such teaching, was not only to present certain facts and methods of study, but also to start a process of independent inquiry and common discussion. I hope that the book can be used in these same ways, for a kind of communication which I believe to be valuable.

I said in *Culture and Society:* 'I shall be glad to be answered, in whatever terms ... When we consider how matters now stand, our continuing interest and language could hardly be too lively.' I have greatly valued the very many answers I actually received, agreeing and disagreeing. The original invitation stands.

2
History

THE printed book is the first great means of modern communication. Writing had made possible the recording of communication; printing made possible its rapid distribution. In England there were two or three printers in 1500, but by 1600 more than ninety. Thirteen titles were printed in 1510, but by 1600 an annual average of about 150. The printing of ballads, almanacs, and pamphlets also increased at a rapid rate. In the seventeenth century the ordinary edition of a book was about 2,000 copies, while a popular almanac sold an average of 16,000 copies.

Between 1500 and 1700 many attempts to regulate printing were made by the State. A form of censorship was set up in 1538; the number of printing houses was several times limited by patent; offending authors were liable to prosecution. These measures fluctuated with a changing political history. As printing moved towards the newspaper, severe measures were taken. In 1662 a Licensing Act limited the number of printers, to prevent 'abuses', and in 1663 a Surveyor of the Press was appointed, with a virtual monopoly in printed news. Parliament's refusal to renew this Licensing Act in 1695 led to a rapid expansion of newspapers and magazines. The history of communications from 1700 until our own century is largely the history of the Press. From the slowly improving postal services to the coming of railways and telegrams, this expansion was dependent on general communications. The use of steam printing, from 1814, decisively raised the rate of distribution, and the effect of subsequent changes in printing, including major changes now taking place, is profound.

By the early nineteenth century, the annual sale of newspapers was about twenty-four million, and some 580 books were published each year, in ordinary editions of about 1,000. Between 1700 and 1820, however, there had been repeated attempts, in new forms, to control what was printed. There was extensive Government bribery of journalists, and certain compliant newspapers were subsidized. Direct State control was replaced by forms of market tax: the Stamp Duty, on every newspaper page, and the Advertisement Tax. These were not to raise revenue but to 'suppress libels'. Starting at a halfpenny in the early eighteenth century, Stamp Duty had risen to fourpence by 1815, the steep rise mainly in the later years, in direct relation to the growth of radical opinion. Independent journalists fought back, even after the further imposition, in 1819, of formal Acts directly aimed at suppressing freedom of expression.

After the Reform Bill of 1832, the situation changed. The tax on advertisements was reduced in 1833 and abolished in 1853. Stamp Duty was reduced in 1836 and abolished in 1855. These developments, aided by the growth of steam printing and railways, led to a further and more rapid expansion. Sales of newspapers rose by 33 per cent between 1816 and 1836, by 70 per cent between 1836 and 1856, and by some 600 per cent between 1856 and 1882. From the 1830s, the new Sunday newspapers, dealing mainly in reports of crime and sensational fiction, took a lead over daily newspapers which they have never lost. By 1850 the daily papers were being read by one adult in eighty, the Sunday papers by one adult in twenty. By 1900 the daily papers were read by one adult in five or six, the Sunday papers by one adult in three. There was a comparable expansion in the reading of magazines, and a slower expansion in the reading of books. The annual production of some 580 books in 1810 had become 2,600 in the 1850s and reached 6,000 by 1901. Editions had become larger and prices were lower.

We must now turn to another line of development, in the theatre and in forms of entertainment. The first theatres were built in England in the 1570s, but there had been a popular drama before this, in the guild plays – miracles and moralities – performed at festivals in the streets and market-places. Beside these, there was a body of popular entertainment, given by travelling professional performers, at fairs and similar occasions, often with difficulty from the law which normally treated them as rogues and vagabonds. The importance of the new theatres of the 1570s was that some of these professionals at last found a home, though the theatres remained under constant pressure from the authorities, and the companies had to seek patronage and protection to survive. Over forty years (then declining before the Puritan closures of the 1640s) there was a remarkable cultural growth, in which the professional actors and the new professional dramatists found a popular audience. Other forms of professional entertainment continued under the usual difficulties.

When the theatres were reopened, in 1660, there was a new kind of division. There were to be only two Royal Patent Theatres, and these were to have a monopoly of what thus came to be called 'legitimate' drama. Other kinds of professional entertainer had survived, and in the eighteenth century, while many continued to tour the fairs, others found their way into new kinds of theatre – the 'illegitimate' world of pantomime, spectacle, and variety. The monopoly of the Patent Theatres was not broken until as late as 1843. It had done much to enforce the idea of two separate traditions of performance, one 'art' and one 'entertainment'. Yet the dividing line had never been clear, and there had been some expansion of theatres.

In 1600, at the height of the Elizabethan drama, there were at least six theatres in London. In 1700, after the narrowing of the Restoration, there were only two. By 1750, five London theatres and five in the provinces had grown up alongside the Patent Theatres, and by 1800 the number in the provinces had reached forty. By 1850 there were twenty-one theatres in London, and seventy-five in the provinces. The real expansion came between 1850 and 1900, and at the end of it there were sixty-three theatres in London and more than 300 in the provinces. Moreover, from the 1840s music-halls had been appearing, developing out of casual entertainment in drinking places. There were forty music-halls by 1900, mainly carrying on parts of the old 'illegitimate' tradition, but now with such new features as high-pressure publicity campaigns and fantastic salaries, and with some new and valuable developments in variety. The old market fairs declined in importance, but the menagerie and the 'horse-riding' developed, by the last quarter of the nineteenth century, into the circus. In the same period, football and racing became parts of organized entertainment, with regular meetings, charges for admission, and many more spectators.

In the 1890s a further series of changes began to appear. In 1896 the first wireless patent was registered and the first cinema show in England took place, later transferring to run in a music-hall. The full effect of the wireless and the cinema did not become apparent until the 1920s, but meanwhile there were very important

25

changes in the organization of the Press. The 'North-cliffe Revolution', as it is usually called, was not the invention of popular journalism; this had begun as early as the Sunday papers of the 1830s and perhaps before. The crucial change made by Northcliffe was in the economic organization of the Press.

Throughout the eighteenth and nineteenth centuries the newspapers had relied, to varying degrees, on some income from advertising. This was at its highest point of importance in the mid eighteenth century, and at its lowest in the second half of the nineteenth century. Such advertisement was mainly of the kind we now call 'classified': specific individual notices. But, outside the Press, other kinds of advertising had been rapidly developing. In its early days it was closely connected with fairs and in particular with the travellers selling patent medicines. Their methods got into print, partly through the newspapers, but more commonly through bills and posters. In the early and middle years of the nineteenth century billposting became a large and organized trade. All kinds of buildings were used, often without consent, and eventually in 1862 special hoardings were organized by the Billposters' Association. Handbills were still given out in extraordinary numbers in the streets, and men and vehicles were hired to parade boards and displays. These became so many that in 1853 the men were officially confined to the gutters and the vehicles were forbidden. New developments followed: skyline and balloon advertisements, larger posters on the new hoardings, electric signs. At last, from the 1880s, the new kinds of display advertising began to break into the Press, at a time when changes in marketing and the development of the retail trade were changing the whole basis of advertising. Northcliffe and similar figures saw increased revenue from the new display advertising as the key to modern newspaper finance, and in particular as a means to reduction in price per copy so as to gain a large circulation. He published his own circulation figures, and challenged his rivals to do the same. The new-style advertising agencies supported this challenge, which was not finally successful until 1931. By this time the whole structure of the nineteenth-century Press had been radically altered. The typical nineteenth-century newspaper, while using advertising revenue, was in no way dependent on it. The typical twentieth-century newspaper became heavily dependent on advertising revenue, to the extent of just under a half of all revenue in the popular newspapers, and some three-quarters of all revenue in the traditional minority newspapers. If, in these different classes of advertising, sufficient revenue cannot be obtained, the typical commercial newspaper is now closed down.

A second part of this major reorganization was the development of groups or chains of newspapers and magazines. The typical form of ownership in the nineteenth century had been by a printer, a printing family, or a small company. It was rare for more than one paper to be owned by the same person or company. But the new kind of owner, such as Northcliffe, Pearson, and Newnes, built up groups of magazines and then went on to start or acquire newspapers. This process has continued all through this century, and newspapers and magazines have nearly all passed from their previous status as independent private enterprises to membership of these new kinds of capitalist combine.

In recent years this process has been accelerating. There seem certain to be further changes, but in 1965 seven out of eight copies of all national morning papers were controlled by three groups (Beaverbrook, King,

Rothermere), while seven out of eight copies of national Sunday papers were controlled by two of these groups (Beaverbrook and King) and a third (*News of the World*). The two London evening papers are controlled by Beaverbrook and Rothermere. A substantial part of the provincial Press belongs to four groups: Rothermere, Thomson, Cowdray, and Drayton. The King group, which controls two out of five copies of all national daily and Sunday papers, has also a virtual monopoly of all large-circulation women's magazines, is the largest single owner of technical and trade journals, and in all controls more than 300 publications.

The expansion of readership in this century has been great. By 1920 one adult in two read a daily paper, while every four adults read five Sunday papers. By 1947, every ten adults read twelve daily papers and twenty-three Sunday papers. At the same time the range of papers available has steadily declined. Where there were nine evening papers in the London area at the end of the nineteenth century there are now only two. Five national daily or Sunday papers have been closed down since the beginning of 1960, and seven provincial morning papers have been closed in the last fifteen years. By comparison with 1900 there is a vastly expanded total readership and a seriously limited range of choice. It is worth pointing out that the papers which have been closed usually had substantial circulations; even very large circulations by all earlier standards. The last available figures for the five national papers which have been closed show sales of over two million (*Empire News*), one and a half million (*Dispatch*), and over one million each (*News Chronicle*, *Graphic*, *Sunday Chronicle*). Such figures show that it cannot be said that these papers had to close because people would not buy them. It is rather that, in modern Press finance, such high actual figures are not high enough to attract the necessary amounts of advertising revenue. Papers with much lower circulations, such as *The Times* and the *Guardian* (about a quarter of a million each), survive because the nature of their readership (people with higher incomes and more social influence) enables them to get advertising revenue at higher rates. So the position is that newspapers do not survive or fail according to how many people want them, but according to their suitability as media for advertising. This is a distinctive feature of this large part of communications in twentieth-century Britain.

The theatre has been steadily declining in the same period. The 400 theatres and music-halls in the country in 1900 have declined to some 200, and the decline is continuing. An important part of this decline is due to competition from cinemas, which created in their turn a new and very large audience. By 1939, the cinema audience in Britain was nineteen million people a week, and by 1946 over thirty-one million. Since the end of the war there has been a decline, rapidly accelerated by the coming of television. By 1956 the weekly audience was down to twenty-one million, by 1959 to eleven and a half million, and by 1964 to eight million. During this post-war decline, more than a half of all cinemas have been closed. In 1952 there were 4,609 cinemas open, in 1959 some 3,450, in 1965 some 2,056. Closures are continuing.

The expansion of the theatre in the nineteenth century, and of the cinema in the twentieth century, show certain common features. In the early phase, in each case, typical ownership was by a small speculator, who gradually built up a local group. In later phases, combines similar to those which emerged in the Press began to be established, especially in the London theatre, in chains of provincial halls, and in the large cinema circuits. In the cinema there has been closely interlocking ownership of both the distributing and the production sides. In decline, both theatres and cinemas have been treated as ordinary commercial property, and have often been closed as part of speculative property schemes.

The characteristic form of ownership of the means of communication in twentieth-century Britain was set aside when broadcasting began to be developed. Perhaps because of its implications for national security, the early development of broadcasting was soon taken over by a public authority from the original trade combine. In 1927 a Royal Charter established the BBC as an independent public corporation, with monopoly rights. This charter was renewed in 1937, and then covered the early development of television. The first public television service had been established by the BBC in 1936. In 1954 the television monopoly was broken, and a second authority, ITA, set up by Act of Parliament. The Independent Television Authority owns its means of transmission, but contracts for the provision of programmes with some thirteen companies. Where the BBC draws its revenue from a proportion of receiving licence fees, the ITA is maintained by payments from the programme companies, which obtain their own revenue from selling advertising time. Thus, by the middle nineteen-fifties, a form very similar to that which had emerged in the Press could be discerned in what became the majority television service. A major part of revenue is derived from advertising, on which the programme companies, like newspapers, are dependent. The element of control by ITA, and by the terms of the Act establishing it, is a differentiating factor. It is significant, in terms of the general situation, that much of the investment in the programme companies has been by the existing newspaper combines, and by similar groups in the theatre and the cinema. There has been a powerful recent campaign to extend this system, with its dependence on advertising revenue, to sound broadcasting.

The growth of audiences, in sound and television, has been spectacular. Between twenty and twenty-five million people watch television each day. The great majority of families have wireless sets, and more than ninety per cent of the population have television in their homes. Audiences for particular programmes are the largest ever known in the history of our communications. An important result of broadcasting has been a notable increase in audiences for musical concerts, and more recently there has been an enormous development in the distribution of records of all kinds, more than seventy-eight million records being produced in Britain in 1964.

In books, also, there has been a major expansion. By 1901 the number of annual titles produced had reached 6,000. By 1924 it was over 12,000, by 1937 over 17,000, and in 1963 it was a total of 26,023, of which 20,367 were first editions. Library facilities have been greatly expanded, and there are now some 460 million loans a year in the Public Library service. The rapidly extending production of paperbacks has greatly increased the number of actual sales, the sale of paperbacks alone having increased from twenty million to more than eighty million a year, between the mid-1950s and the mid-1960s. In general, rather more than fifteen books a year are read per head of population. The actual book-reading public seems to be nearly sixty per cent of the population (of course with great unevenness as to actual use). This majority public for books was probably first achieved in the 1950s, by comparison with a majority public for Sunday papers by 1910 and for daily papers by the end of the First World War.

The production of books seems to be undergoing similar changes of ownership to those noted for the Press at the end of the nineteenth century. There are still many independent publishers, but there is also a marked tendency towards combine ownership, and already a considerable number of apparently independent imprints have been absorbed into large publishing groups.

What can we learn from this general record? It is clear that there are two major factors in the modern history of communications. There is, first, the remarkable expansion of audiences. In newspapers, magazines, books, broadcasting, television, and recorded music there has been an expansion beyond any previous conception, and this is still continuing. The recent decline in the cinema audience still leaves a very large public, and the decline in the theatre can be offset by this expansion, and especially by the great increase in audiences for drama through broadcasting and television. The whole process has the effect of a cultural revolution.

At the same time, there has been another major development. The ownership of the means of communication, old and new, has passed or is passing, in large part, to a kind of financial organization unknown in earlier periods, and with important resemblances to the major forms of ownership in general industrial production. The methods and attitudes of capitalist business have established themselves near the centre of communications. There is the widespread dependence on advertising money, which leads to a policy of getting a large audience as quickly as possible, to attract and hold advertisers. From this it becomes one of the major purposes of communication to sell a particular paper or programme. All the basic purposes of communication – the sharing of human experience – can become subordinated to this drive to sell.

The pressure here is actually increasing. The old kind of newspaper proprietor, who wanted control so that he could propagate his opinions, is being replaced by a kind of proprietor who says he is not interested in opinions but simply in selling as many papers as he can. What was once a means to some larger policy has become in many cases the policy itself. The organization of communications is then not for use, but for profit, and we seem to have passed the stage in which there has to be any pretence that things are otherwise.

This emphasis inevitably extends into the substance of communication. It is bound to remain a human world, in some form; it can never be only the production of things. But methods learned from the selling of things can be applied to persons. There can be a kind of manufacture and marketing of personalities, as in the powerful and expanding world of publicity. There can also be a kind of packaging of experience: putting it out with the right gloss, or even making the gloss a substitute for the experience. The human effects of such tendencies are bound to be serious, but attention to them can be dismissed as 'idealism' while the emphasis on selling is seen as normal and practical. The irony is that the only practical use of communication is the sharing of real experience. To set anything above this is in fact quite unpractical. To set selling above it may seem normal, but is really only a perversion to which some people have got used: a way of looking at the world which must be right and normal because you have cut yourself down to its size.

The interaction between these two major processes – the popular expansion and the emphasis on selling – is extremely complicated. The two are tied together in our minds, because they happened together. It is difficult to see that things might have been otherwise, can still be otherwise.

The correct historical analysis is twofold. First, it is clear that the extension of communications has been part of the extension of democracy. Yet, in this century, while the public has extended, ownership and control of the means of communication have narrowed. There is fear of public control because of the memories of State control in the past, but control can be of many kinds. In the modern combine system there is a new kind of control, and we might agree with Burke that

wise men will apply their remedies to vices, not to names . . . Otherwise you will be wise historically, a fool in practice . . . You are terrifying yourself with ghosts and apparitions, whilst your house is the haunt of robbers.

In the modern trend towards limited ownership, the cultural conditions of democracy are in fact being denied: sometimes, ironically, in the name of freedom.

Second, it is clear that the expansion has been and is a process of human growth. All growth is difficult, and needs time and care. Many kinds of confusion and uncertainty are inevitably encountered. If the attempt is made to preserve old forms intact, and to denounce the new in their name, the old forms simply become irrelevant to the new problems. What can then happen is that control of the new forms passes to men who are not interested in the growth of the society, or in the human purposes the expansion is serving. Such men will see inexperience as an opportunity, and confusion

34

as a sanction. Instead of a new culture emerging, a synthetic culture – meeting and exploiting the tensions of growth – will be devised for a quick sale. While such men rule, there will indeed be expansion but there will be no real growth.

A synthetic culture is easy. An old culture is remote. We are caught in this tension, yet the forces of growth, the real drives of the expansion, cannot in the end be denied. Already, through many difficulties, there has been growth of a real and valuable kind. But the nature of the expansion warns us that we cannot apply any simple overall test. We have to recognize the contradictions we have been following: between democracy and limited ownership; between genuine extension and the drive to sell. The real history of communications, in showing us the contradictions, shows us also the need to choose between genuinely alternative directions for the future.

3
Content

WE get used to particular papers and programmes and often, after a while, come to take their typical content for granted. Some degree of familiarity with a particular paper or programme is indeed often necessary, if what it has to offer is to come through to us easily. But of course there is a danger, as we get used to the particular way of looking at the world which our favourite paper or programme embodies, that we shall forget that it is, after all, only one of many possible ways. Most of us realize that the worlds seen by *The Times* and by the *Daily Mirror*, or by the Third Programme and by an ITV programme company, are in certain basic ways different. But to know only these general and obvious differences is not enough. If we are to be really alert and independent, as in a democracy we ought to be, we have to look critically at the content and methods we are used to as well as those which we have decided are not our kind. There are several ways in which we can make this examination for ourselves. I want to illustrate some of them, both to show possible methods and to give some actual material. This kind of examination needs to be carried out regularly, not only so that we can keep in touch with important changes (which are often not announced), but also so that we can make historical comparisons and discern particular trends. Also, there is always some error in sampling, and this can only be reduced if other samples are taken and if many people are carrying out the examination. Where similar work has been done previously, I have kept as far as possible to procedures which allow comparisons. But such work has been scattered and irregular, and I have tried to introduce some new kinds. I will set this work out in three sections: first, measurement by categories of content; second, analysis of style and presentation; third, comparative survey.

MEASUREMENT BY CATEGORIES

Here I propose to look at a sample of newspapers, magazines, and programmes, in terms of the proportions of space and time given to different categories of material. I begin with the Press, and with national morning newspapers in particular. I want to look first at the division of available space into advertising and all other (editorial) material. Table 1 sets out the results of a sample analysis; the price, number of pages, and average circulation of the papers are included to see what relation they may have to the advertising and editorial figures.

Table 1 (a)

July 1961	Price in pence	Pages	Average circulation in thousands	Percentage editorial material	Percentage advertising material
Times	5	18	260	68	32
Guardian	4	16	235	61	39
Telegraph	3	22	1,264	52	48
Mail	3	16	2,687	68	32
Express	3	12	4,313	66	34
Herald	3	10	1,418	77	23
Worker	3	4	?	97	3
Mirror	3	20*	4,593	67	33
Sketch	3	16*	1,000	90	10

*Tabloid size.

The division of space between advertising and editorial material is not, then, governed by whether a paper is 'quality' or 'popular'. The three papers with the lowest proportions of advertising, the *Herald*, *Sketch*, and *Worker*, would certainly include more if they could get it. The *Herald* and *Sketch* get less because by comparison with their immediate competitors their circulations are low. *The Times* and *Guardian*, with lower circulations, get relatively more advertising because the social and economic standing of their readers attracts advertisers. The *Worker* gets very little advertising because of its political policy combined with its small circulation. When these exceptions are allowed for, we get an average figure of roughly one third of all available space being given to advertising.

A further sample analysis, for comparison and continuity, was made in 1965.

Table 1 (b)

July 1965	Price in pence	Pages	Average circulation in thousands	Percentage editorial material	Percentage advertising material
Times	6	24	258	64	36
Guardian	5	22	276	63	37
Telegraph	4	32	1,351	44	56
Mail	3	16	2,425	61	39
Express	4	16	4,042	61	39
Sun	4	14	1,361	69	31
Worker	4	4	60	96	4
Mirror	4	24*	4,957	65	35
Sketch	4	20*	826	80	20

*Tabloid size.

The most evident change in these later figures is a slight but significant increase in the percentage of advertising in nearly all daily newspapers (the *Worker* remains an exception for the reasons previously given). The average percentage for all papers in 1961 was 28 per cent; for all other than the *Worker*, 31 per cent. By 1965 these percentages had increased respectively to 33 per cent and 36 per cent.

Among particular changes, the increase in advertising in the *Telegraph*, to its present remarkable figure, and the continued relative weakness of the *Sun* (replacing the *Herald*) and the *Sketch*, are notable. Overall circulation has remained steady, though with some interesting minor movements between papers.

The dependence of newspapers on a substantial proportion of advertising has been normal since the period between the wars. If we look at the percentage of advertising space in three typical papers over a period, we find:

	1937	1955	1961	1965
Times	33	40	32	36
Mail	41	36	32	39
Mirror	26	34	33	35

Whether the paper is, in conventional terms, 'quality', 'popular' or 'tabloid', a comparable dependence on commercial advertising can be seen, in our period, to be a common characteristic.

However, advertising is a very general category. If we look at the use of advertising space, we find some important differences between kinds of paper. For example, some papers have a high proportion of classified advertisements (specific notices, usually in ordinary size type); others a high proportion of display advertisements (usually very general and persuasive in tone, using illustrations and often very large type). In

39

Table 2 there are some sample percentages. We can usually spot these marked differences simply by looking at the papers concerned. But there are other differences, in the use of advertising space, which have to be more carefully examined. It is worth picking out certain classes of goods and services, to see what proportions of space they get in different papers. A sample distribution is shown in Table 3.

This is the distribution of *display* advertising only, leaving aside the different proportions of classified and display already noted. Obviously there are variations in these percentages, from time to time, but some general points are very clear. Most important, perhaps, is the category described as 'inter-company and public opinion' advertising, which on its present scale is a comparatively new development. Such advertisements aim at no direct or (for most people) conceivable buying. The products they advertise could only be bought by quite large organizations, and often only by quite specialized trades. Why then advertise in a general newspaper rather than a trade periodical? The usual explanation is that the newspapers actually used for this kind of advertising have among their readers the highest proportions of people in a position to make such large buying decisions, and this is obviously true so far as it goes. Yet such proportions must be quite small, by comparison with the actual proportions of space. The explanation seems to be that, quite apart from any actual business promoted by these advertisements, the prestige or 'image' of the company is promoted among readers held to be particularly influential in leading public opinion. In bulk, such advertising seems also to promote the 'image' of modern business as a whole. The borderline between this and straight political advertising is often quite difficult to see.

Table 2 (a)

July 1961	Times	Guardian	Telegraph	Mail	Express	Herald	Worker	Mirror	Sketch
Classified	69	66	85	12	13	27	34	9	19
Display	31	34	15	88	87	73	66	91	81

Table 2 (b)

July 1965	Times	Guardian	Telegraph	Mail	Express	Sun	Worker	Mirror	Sketch
Classified	77	75	73	44	22	18	100	9	41
Display	23	25	27	56	78	82	0	91	59

Table 3 (a)

July 1961	Inter-company and public opinion	Travel	Cars	Drink and tobacco	Other consumer goods	Food	Patent medicines	Miscellaneous
Times	57	10	8	8	5	—	1	11
Guardian	48	7	8	9	18	—	1	9
Telegraph	37	9	8	6	28	1	8	3
Mail	—	2	2	13	55	10	9	9
Express	—	2	2	14	43	10	16	13
Herald	—	—	—	3	62	9	13	13
Worker	—	—	—	—	100	—	—	—
Mirror	—	—	—	13	59	9	16	3
Sketch	—	—	—	42	25	—	7	26

Table 3 (b)

July 1965	Inter-company and public opinion	Travel	Cars	Drink and tobacco	Other consumer goods	Food	Patent medicines	Miscellaneous
Times	76	24	—	—	—	—	—	—
Guardian	63	14	11	—	12	—	—	—
Telegraph	54	8	14	7	9	8	—	—
Mail	—	—	7	31	20	37	2	3
Express	—	—	14	2	22	38	7	17
Sun	—	—	—	25	18	31	$\frac{1}{2}$	$25\frac{1}{2}$
Worker	—	—	—	—	—	—	—	—
Mirror	—	—	—	22	39	19	19	1
Sketch	—	8	—	14	8	42	24	4

The distribution of display advertising forms a reasonably clear pattern, with the more expensive goods and services, notably travel and cars, more heavily advertised in the more expensive papers, or those reaching readers with most money. Distribution of the middle range of display advertising is less significant: the local variations in these particular samples are not particularly important, and further sampling would undoubtedly amend them. But just as the significant feature of display in the more expensive papers is the crucial 'inter-company and public opinion' category, so one significant feature of display in the cheaper range is the distribution of patent medicine advertising, which seems to be concentrated in the papers reaching the poorest and least educated members of the community. This apparently conscious policy needs the most careful and continuing observation.

I have dealt so far only with the use of advertising space. I have done this because it is part of the content of a paper which can so easily be overlooked, although it is a very important part both in size and style. I turn now to the use of the remaining space, usually about two-thirds of the paper. There is a sample distribution of percentages in Table 4 (a). The classification used in this table follows that in Appendix VII of the Report of the Royal Commission on the Press, 1947–9. The categories are self-explanatory, except for 'miscellaneous', which includes cartoons and puzzles. The differences between various papers stand out quite clearly. Most notable, perhaps, is the high proportion of cartoon and similar material, and the low proportion of news, in the two 'tabloid' papers, *Mirror* and *Sketch*. In proportions given to pictures, there are less differences now than there once were, when the term 'picture-paper' could indicate a distinct kind. A difference in use and kind of picture will be noted later.

Table 4 (a)

July 1961	News	Features	Leaders	Letters	Pictures	Miscellaneous
Times	74	8	3	$2\frac{1}{2}$	11	$1\frac{1}{2}$
Guardian	64	17	3	3	10	3
Telegraph	61	18	2	3	14	2
Mail	55	$8\frac{1}{2}$	1	1	$25\frac{1}{2}$	9
Express	62	8	1	1	18	10
Herald	64	9	2	2	14	9
Worker	70	12	3	1	12	2
Mirror	45	7	1	2	29	16
Sketch	49	7	1	2	18	23

It is worth noting that the proportion of news, in contemporary newspapers, is not always very high. Indeed, if we take it as a proportion of the total material (including advertising) printed, the highest figure is that of the *Worker*, at some sixty-eight per cent (a misleading figure in some ways, because of the very small amount of advertising included), while the other papers range from the fifty per cent of *The Times* to the thirty per cent of the *Mirror*. But we must bring to these figures a further analysis, if we are to assess content accurately. We must look at the proportions of total news space given to particular kinds of news. A sample distribution of percentages is given in Table 5 (a).

Table 5 (a)

July 1961	International, political, social and economic	Domestic political, social and economic	Law, police, and accidents	Personalities	Sport	Arts including radio and television	Financial and Commercial	Miscellaneous
Times	18	11	1	6	23	10	28	3
Guardian	21	19	1	1	28	12	15	3
Telegraph	21	$14\frac{1}{2}$	$3\frac{1}{2}$	5	$34\frac{1}{2}$	9	11	$1\frac{1}{2}$
Mail	9	12	12	8	35	8	9	7
Express	16	13	17	3	42	2	2	5
Herald	11	15	9	12	43	6	3	1
Worker	19	38	1	—	29	10	—	3
Mirror	5	13	14	17	38	2	—	11
Sketch	2	9	14	17	36	3	3	16

The differences here are very interesting, and repay careful study. Here, especially, pictures of the world – selections of things worth attending to – are formed and communicated. We must not of course make the mistake of assuming that the only serious news is that

classified as 'political, social, and economic'; there are
many other kinds of human fact which can be serious
news. Yet the Press is so often discussed in terms of this
one function, giving the facts necessary for political,
social, and economic judgement in a democracy, that it
is worth noting not only the differences between papers,
but the actual proportions in any and all. If we take
political, social, and economic news, both international
and domestic, as a proportion of the total material
(including advertising) printed, the highest figure is the
rather special case of the *Worker*, with thirty-nine per
cent, while the other papers range from around sixteen
per cent, for *The Times* and the *Guardian*, to the lowest
figure of about five per cent in the *Sketch*. These are
quite startling figures, by comparison with our usual
assumptions about the main functions of our newspapers.

A later analysis gives the following tables for
comparison.

Table 4 (b)

July 1965	News	Features	Leaders	Letters	Pictures	Misc.
Times	79	$7\frac{1}{2}$	$2\frac{1}{2}$	2	$7\frac{1}{2}$	2
Guardian	66	20	$2\frac{1}{2}$	$1\frac{1}{2}$	6	4
Telegraph	67	19	2	1	9	2
Mail	$63\frac{1}{2}$	13	1	$\frac{1}{2}$	10	12
Express	67	8	1	2	9	13
Sun	63	$12\frac{1}{2}$	$2\frac{1}{4}$	$2\frac{1}{4}$	10	10
Worker	67	13	3	—	10	7
Mirror	63	5	1	3	12	16
Sketch	51	$13\frac{1}{2}$	$1\frac{1}{2}$	1	18	15

Table 5 (b)

July 1965	International political, social and economic	Domestic political, social and economic	Law, police, and accidents	Personalities	Sport	Arts including radio and television	Financial and Commercial	Miscellaneous
Times	13	$23\frac{1}{2}$	5	6	$15\frac{1}{2}$	$7\frac{1}{2}$	28	$1\frac{1}{2}$
Guardian	$19\frac{1}{2}$	31	$4\frac{1}{2}$	1	9	21	14	—
Telegraph	7	29	4	4	23	16	17	—
Mail	14	24	5	10	31	4	12	—
Express	4	$14\frac{1}{2}$	10	10	$52\frac{1}{2}$	2	7	—
Sun	$4\frac{1}{2}$	$33\frac{1}{2}$	$14\frac{1}{2}$	3	$32\frac{1}{2}$	2	9	1
Worker	8	47	4	—	34	7	—	—
Mirror	2	22	26	14	31	4	1	—
Sketch	2	19	13	15	49	1	1	—

The most interesting change to emerge from these later figures is a steady increase, in almost all papers, in the amount of space given to news. In the case of the *Mirror* this is a marked increase. By comparison, the space given to pictures is in almost all cases reduced. It is too early to say whether this is a settled trend, but so far as it goes it is encouraging. This is, however, a change in the distribution of editorial matter only, and is masked by the increase in advertising noted earlier. Thus, if we take news as a proportion of the total material (including advertising) printed, the highest figure is again that of the *Worker* (still a special case, because of the very low proportion of advertising), while the other papers range from the forty-nine per cent of *The Times* to the thirty per cent of the *Telegraph* (a figure obviously affected by the very high proportion of advertising) and of the *Express*. This range is very similar to that in 1961, with minor changes between particular papers. Again, if we take political, social and economic news, both international and domestic, as a proportion of the total material (including advertising) printed, the highest figure is again the special case of the *Worker*, at thirty-five per cent, while the other papers range from twenty-three per cent in the *Guardian*, through a mean of seventeen per cent, to nine per cent in the *Mirror* and seven per cent in the *Express*. These are rather better figures than in 1961, but the low figures for the two most widely selling papers are disturbing. Moreover, the distribution of news coverage between domestic and international events turns out, on analysis, to be even more disturbing. The sample was taken during an important phase of the international crisis in Vietnam, yet the highest figure for international news (from all material printed) is eight per cent in the *Guardian*, and is below one per cent in the *Sketch*. Here too, we might say, by selection and emphasis, pictures of the world are decisively and perhaps disastrously formed.

Table 6

1965	Price	Pages	% Editorial	% Advertising	% Political, Social and Economic News
Times	6	24	64	36	19
Guardian	5	22	63	37	23
Telegraph	4	32	44	56	12
Le Monde	7†	24*	82	18	72
Die Welt	8†	22	51	49	33
La Stampa	6†	18	51	49	27

†Price to nearest penny, at normal exchange rate.
*Tabloid size.

A brief comparison of the space given to editorial and advertising material, and of the percentage of all space given to international and domestic political, social and economic news, can be made between the three English 'quality' papers and three directly comparable papers in France, West Germany and Italy (see Table 6).

We can turn next to the Sunday papers, for some comparative figures. In Table 7 there is a sample distribution between editorial and advertising space, with the relevant figures for price, size, and circulation.

The proportions of space given to advertising are generally rather higher in the Sunday papers. The one really low figure, for *Reynolds News* in 1961 and for its successor the *Sunday Citizen* in 1965, is related to low circulation and perhaps its political policy. The division of the percentage of space between classified and display advertising, given in Table 8, reveals a very similar pattern to that in the national morning Press, though there has been an increase in classified advertising in the more popular Sunday papers.

Table 7 (a)

July 1961	Price in pence	Pages	Average circulation in thousands	Percentage editorial material	Percentage advertising material
S. Times	6	36	1,023	51	49
Observer	6	32	733	54	46
S. Telegraph	5	28	716	67	33
S. Express	5	28	3,767	51	49
People	5	18	5,442	60	40
News of World	5	16	6,734	67	33
Reynolds News	5	14	326	81	19
Pictorial	5	28*	5,335	70	30

*Tabloid size.

Table 7 (b)

July 1965	Price in pence	Pages	Average circulation in thousands	Percentage editorial material	Percentage advertising material
S. Times	8	46+36*	1,275	47	53
Observer	7	32+32*	829	53	47
S. Telegraph	6	24	662	74	26
S. Express	6	24	4,187	55	45
People	6	20	5,509	60	40
News of World	6	18	6,175	65	35
S. Citizen	6	32*	236	84	16
S. Mirror	6	36*	5,022	66	34

*Tabloid size.

Table 8 (a)

July 1961	*Sunday Times*	*Observer*	*Sunday Telegraph*	*Sunday Express*	*People*	*News of the World*	*Reynolds News*	*Sunday Pictorial*
Classified	56	56	38	8	1	3	2	1
Display	44	44	62	92	99	97	98	99

Table 8 (b)

July 1965	Sunday Times	Observer	Sunday Telegraph	Sunday Express	People	News of the World	Sunday Citizen	Sunday Mirror
Classified	63	61	68	23	21	20	20	12
Display	37	39	32	77	79	80	80	88

There are also important resemblances in the distribution of display advertising space for certain goods and services, as is shown by Table 9.

Table 9 (a)

July 1961	Inter-company and public opinion	Travel	Cars	Drink and tobacco	Other consumer goods	Food	Patent medicines	Miscellaneous
Sunday Times	39	8	23	2	12	—	—	16
Observer	20	9	17	8	24	—	—	22
Sunday Telegraph	11	5	39	3	26	8	1	7
Sunday Express	6	4	24	12	35	1	3	15
People	6	3	6	14	31	6	14	20
News of the World	7	—	3	9	40	10	23	8
Reynolds News	13	—	14	3	15	41	2	12
Pictorial	—	1	6	18	52	7	9	7

Table 9 (*b*)

July 1965	Inter-company and public opinion	Travel	Cars	Drink and tobacco	Other consumer goods	Food	Patent medicines	Miscellaneous
Sunday Times	22	7	7	14	29	3	2	16
Observer	13	15	14	20	17	—	—	21
Sunday Telegraph	—	16	26	—	12	17	3	26
Sunday Express	—	10	14	9	25	11	4	27
People	—	1	4	24	37	8	19	7
News of the World	—	1	29	14	27	—	16	13
Sunday Citizen	—	3	—	—	40	42	13	2
Sunday Mirror	—	4	2	15	41	2	12	24

Here the importance of inter-company and public opinion advertising, in certain papers, is again clear, as is also the concentration of patent medicine advertising. The distribution of other display advertising follows the now characteristic pattern.

When we turn to the use of editorial space, we find important differences. A sample distribution of percentages is given in Table 10 (a).

It is now an established feature of the Sunday Press that it gives more of its space to features of all kinds, and correspondingly less to news, than the national morning papers.

Only the *News of the World* prints as large a proportion of news as most of the morning papers, and this is rather a special case. We can only interpret these figures adequately if we analyse kinds of news. A sample

Table *10 (a)*

July 1961	News	Features	Leaders	Letters	Pictures	Miscellaneous
Sunday Times	50	24	5	3	14	4
Observer	49	25	5	3	11	7
Sunday Telegraph	55	22	3	2	14	4
Sunday Express	40	30	1	1	20	8
People	52	23	2	2	13	8
News of the World	67	12	1	1	6	13
Reynolds News	50	28	2	3	14	3
Pictorial	50	18	1	1	24	6

Table *11 (a)*

July 1961	International political, social, and economic	Domestic political, social, and economic	Law, police, and accidents	Personalities	Sport	Arts	Financial and commercial	Miscellaneous
Sunday Times	10	7	1	9	28	30	12	3
Observer	15	17	1	6	22	35	4	—
Sunday Telegraph	12	9	2	3	31	28	12	3
Sunday Express	8	4	11	11	35	2	11	18
People	1	4	38	4	45	2	—	6
News of the World	9	5	36	5	39	1	3	2
Reynolds News	11	10	8	6	40	17	2	6
Pictorial	4	7	13	11	51	4	—	10

distribution of percentages is set out in Table 11 (a).

It will be seen that whereas news of law cases, police investigations, and accidents exceeded international and domestic political, social, and economic news in only one national morning paper, there is an excess of this kind in three Sunday papers, and in two of them – the *People* and the *News of the World* – it is very marked. Sports news exceeds political, social, and economic news in five out of nine morning papers; in Sunday papers it does so in all but one case. The share of space given to all political, social, and economic news, in the total material (including advertising) printed, varies from the highest figures of between eight per cent and nine per cent in the *Observer* and *Reynolds News* to the lowest of under two per cent in the *People*. There is an even wider variation in the share of space given to news of the arts (books, films, plays, television, radio, music, etc.), from 9·5 per cent in the *Observer* to between 0·4 per cent and 0·5 per cent in the *Sunday Express* and the *News of the World*.

A later sample analysis has been made, for comparison and continuity.

Table 10 (b)

July 1965	News	Features	Leaders	Letters	Pictures	Misc.
Sunday Times	46	25	1	2	23	3
Observer	39	20	2	2	29	8
Sunday Telegraph	63	19	1	2	10	5
Sunday Express	52	23	1	2	13	9
People	61	20	1	4	11	3
News of the World	60	14	1	1	14	10
Sunday Citizen	46	12	1	4	16	21
Sunday Mirror	47	25	—	3	23	2

The generally low figures, for news, by comparison with the morning papers, are confirmed in this later analysis, with minor shifts between papers. The most striking change in the editorial content of the Sunday papers is in the colour supplements of the *Sunday Times* and *Observer*, which have the effect of markedly raising the proportion of space given to pictures. It is noticeable that the advertising photographs and the editorial photographs, in these colour supplements, are very similar in kind and style, to the point where it can require close inspection to distinguish between them at all. By no means all editorial photographs, in the Sunday papers generally, are news photographs, as a look at the *News of the World* or the *Sunday Mirror*, among others, will show. But it is in the colour supplements that a new editorial method is evident, the feature photographs combining with the advertising photographs to present an overall style, evidently intended to suggest what might be called (with an effort) a way of life. This combination of advertising and feature techniques is new only in the sense that it is now, for the first time in this form, entering newspapers. It has been familiar for some years in the women's magazines, from which, as a journalistic method, the colour supplements evidently derive. The high figure for miscellaneous material, including strips and cartoons, in the would-be popular *Sunday Citizen*, is also notable.

In the distribution of editorial attention, some interesting changes may be seen in Table 11 (b).

In this later sample, news of law cases, police investigations and accidents exceeded international and domestic political, social and economic news in only one

Table 11 (b)

July 1965	International political, social, and economic	Domestic political, social, and economic	Law, police, and accidents	Personalities	Sport	Arts	Financial and commercial	Miscellaneous
Sunday Times	13	10	2	6	21	20	25	3
Observer	14	15	1	7	27	25	9	2
Sunday Telegraph	10	17	3	1	31	16	20	2
Sunday Express	11	19	6	10	37	3	10	4
People	1	33	4	14	38	4	1	5
News of the World	2	10	32	13	38	2	2	1
Sunday Citizen	7	31	2	16	32	9	2	1
Sunday Mirror	12	23	7	6	40	1	4	7

Sunday paper, as it also did in only one morning paper. This is an interesting change. Again, in the later sample, sports news exceeds political, social and economic news in three out of nine morning papers, and in five out of eight Sunday papers. There has been some change here, though the distribution of attention still needs emphasis. The share of space given to all news, in Sunday papers, in the total material (including advertising) printed, varies from forty-five per cent in the *Telegraph* to twenty-one per cent in the *Sunday Times* and *Observer*, these two now being at the bottom of this table as a result of their increasing function as feature magazines. The share of space given to all political, social and economic news, in the total material printed, ranges from the sixteen per cent of the *Citizen* (a special case because of its low advertising content) and then from twelve per cent in the *Telegraph* and *People* to six per cent in the *Observer* and five per cent in the *Sunday Times* and *News of the World*. These altered distributions of emphasis, in what were once the traditional 'quality' papers, need careful note. The distribution of news about the arts is again somewhat lower in the later sample, ranging from some six per cent in the *Observer* to 0·6 per cent in the *Sunday Mirror*. On the other hand, the share of space given to financial and commercial news has markedly risen. This category is distinguished from international or domestic economic news by its particular emphasis, which is news of companies and share prices as a guide to private investments, rather than news and analysis, of a general kind, in these fields. In two papers, this financial and commercial news exceeds all international political, social and economic news, and in one case it exceeds both international and domestic political, social and economic news. The pictures of the world, of issues requiring attention, that are being formed here are of great characteristic interest. One other change in a particular paper, that should be noted, is the very marked drop in news of police cases and accidents in *The People*, which in 1961 was directly comparable in this category with the *News of the World* but which now prints a relatively high proportion of domestic social news, including popular surveys and investigations. The low quantity of international news, again during a serious phase of an international crisis, is as marked in the Sunday as in the morning papers. The proportional range is from some eight per cent in the *Sunday Telegraph* to less than one per cent in *The People* and the *News of the World*.

We can complete this account of the use of space in newspapers by looking briefly at the two surviving London evening papers. Tables, 12, 13, and 14 are set out for comparison.

Table 12 (a)

July 1961	Price in pence	Pages	Average circulation in thousands	Percentage editorial material	Percentage advertising material	Classified as percentage of advertising	Display as percentage of advertising
News	3	16	1,486	51	49	58	42
Standard	3	28*	761	48	52	59	41

*Tabloid size.

Table 12 (b)

July 1965	Price in pence	Pages	Average circulation in thousands	Percentage editorial material	Percentage advertising material	Classified as percentage of advertising	Display as percentage of advertising
News	4	18	1,278	37	63	77	23
Standard	4	32*	680	46	54	76	24

*Tabloid size.

Table 13 (a)

July 1961	News	Features	Leaders	Letters	Pictures	Miscellaneous
News	59	13	1	1	14	12
Standard	$61\frac{1}{2}$	11	1	1	$15\frac{1}{2}$	10

Table 13 (b)

July 1965	News	Features	Leaders	Letters	Pictures	Miscellaneous
News	$58\frac{1}{2}$	$15\frac{1}{2}$	1	1	13	11
Standard	61	14	1	2	12	10

Table 14 (a)

July 1961	International political, social and economic	Domestic political, social and economic	Law, police and accidents	Personalities	Sport	Arts	Financial and commercial	Miscellaneous
News	1	18	11	9	36	3	16	6
Standard	$3\frac{1}{2}$	18	8	12	29	3	24	$2\frac{1}{2}$

Table 14 (b)

July 1965	International political, social and economic	Domestic political, social and economic	Law, police and accidents	Personalities	Sport	Arts	Financial and commercial	Miscellaneous
News	1	11	7	19	20	12	18	12
Standard	5	18	15	8	31	3	13	7

We can now see certain general patterns in the distribution of space in newspapers of different kinds. We can go on to look at the same questions in some other important sections of the Press.

The magazines specially published for women and girls are now very important in forming pictures of the world. In most of them the content of advertising is high (see Table 15).

Table 15 (a)

July 1961	Price in pence	Published	Pages	Percentage editorial material	Percentage advertising material
Woman's Own	6	weekly	76	52	48
Woman's Mirror	6	weekly	48	68	32
She	15	monthly	80	58	42
Vogue	30	monthly	110	54	46
*Honey**	18	monthly	68	68	32
*Boyfriend**	5	weekly	28	89	11

Table 15 (b)

July 1965	Price in pence	Published	Pages	Percentage editorial material	Percentage advertising material
Woman's Own	8	weekly	60	59	41
Woman's Mirror	6	weekly	48	70	30
She	24	monthly	100	63	37
Vogue	36	monthly	108	62	38
Honey*	24	monthly	68	54	46
Boyfriend*	9	weekly	32	83	17

The magazines named are examples of each of the main kinds. The two marked * are mainly for adolescent girls. It is often not easy to separate advertising from editorial material. It is not only that the styles of presentation in each are remarkably similar. It is also that a good deal of more or less direct advertising is normally included in certain editorial features. Analysis of content is not easy, but Table 16 (a) shows a sample distribution of interests.

The variations here are interesting, from the preponderance of fiction and gossip in the cheaper magazines to the emphasis on 'buying advice' in the more expensive (the sections on arts and travel in the latter are in some ways simply 'buying advice'). Perhaps more important, however, than these individual variations, is the general exclusion from most of these magazines of all reference to public affairs. The 'non-political' world which this exclusion creates is, however, not without its clear social values, of consumption, personal competition, and (as we shall see when we look more closely at the fiction) social success.

Table 16 (a)

July 1961	Editorial comment	House and cooking	Shopping guide	Personal appearance	Advice on behaviour	Letters	Fiction	Gossip	Medical	Arts	Travel	Children	Animals	Careers
Woman's Own	10	11	1	14	6	3	38	12	2	3	—	—	—	—
Woman's Mirror	10	5	6	11	—	4	15	36	7	1	—	5	—	—
She	17	6	17	3	3	4	6	13	1	8	14	2	6	—
Vogue	5	6	49	10	—	—	—	7	—	19	4	—	—	—
Honey*	10	—	1	21	7	4	26	11	2	6	8	—	—	4
Boyfriend*	5	—	—	8	13	—	47	25	—	2	—	—	—	—

Table 16 (b)

July 1965	Pictures	Editorial material	House and cooking	Shopping guide	Personal appearance	Advice	Letters	Fiction	Gossip	Medical	Arts	Travel	Children	Animals	Careers
Woman's Own	42	—	12½	1½	15	13½	5	29	3	3	1	—	7½	9	—
Woman's Mirror	38½	12	10½	1	7	2½	7	24	23	2	—	9	2	—	—
She	52½	4	9	8½	5	8½	3	10	8	4	12	5	7	1	15
Vogue	75	5	23	13	8	6	—	—	—	—	25	20	—	—	—
Honey*	51	14½	—	7	12	14½	2	34	6½	—	2½	—	—	—	7
Boyfriend*	32	6	—	3½	10	5½	2	60†	8	—	5	—	—	—	—

†83% of this fiction is in strip cartoon form.

A later sample has been taken for continuity. Its categories are the same as in the earlier sample except that a new category, of pictures, has been included, because of its importance in this type of magazine. The figure for pictures is a percentage of all editorial material; the remaining figures, showing distribution of interests, are percentages of editorial material excluding pictures (see Table 16 (b)).

Certain general observations can be made about this analysis. By comparison with the earlier sample, it seems that the interests represented in women's magazines are significantly broadening. It is not only that there are occasional articles of general public interest, but that a magazine like *She*, for example, within its woman's magazine make-up, is in some ways comparable to older kinds of general interest picture magazines. In the same direction, advice on behaviour, which was normally confined to discussion of problems of emotional relationships, now adds to this still substantial emphasis a new kind of advice on legal and financial problems (one feature, for example, is called 'Finance for Females'). In another sense, of course, certain of the magazines consist almost entirely of advice on behaviour, through a very wide range of approaches and techniques. Significantly, it is often difficult to separate such advice on behaviour from the most detailed kind of shopping guide. A special comment is necessary on such magazines as *Vogue* and *Honey*. In *Vogue*, of course, every other interest is subordinated to the display of clothes, but what is most remarkable is an extraordinary integration of other interests into this emphasis. Travel interest, for example, is absorbed into the photographs of clothes, with an emphasis that the background is 'real desert' (place indicated). Being in that place and having those clothes (shopnames and prices overprinted) are decisively brought together. But buying the clothes is an entry to more than this: a *Vogue* feature on picnics, for example, begins with three to four hundred words of an article on picnics in history and art, continues at the back of the magazine where it runs among the advertisements, but continues also in another form in seventeen and a half pages of pictures; reproduction of part of Tissot's painting, *The Picnic*, and then staged photographs putatively illustrating famous picnics in literature, from Dryden's *All for Love* – Cleopatra on the Nile, 'shimmering seductive silk tunic, Eastern blue fringed with golden lace, flowering pearly gold and silver roses; 55 gns. . . . Nile picnic prepared by the New Winter Palace Hotel, Luxor' – to Oscar Wilde – a group in the woods, with precise shopping details not only of the clothes but of the birdcage which happens to be hanging in one of the trees. The reader is offered the art, the quotations, the little article, the clothes, the accessories, the photographs, the authors' names and the travel in a single operation. *Honey* has a further variation of this: an abridged story, called 'A Dream of a Holiday', which runs through seventeen pages, mainly of pictures illustrating episodes in the story ('a package holiday with . . . I hoped, a package romance thrown in'), in which the clothes worn by the characters are on the same page given shop and price details. The reorganisation of wide areas of interest around advertising and a shopping guide has now gone very far indeed. At the same time, a way of life and values belonging to this same integration are tirelessly projected. In *Honey*, for example, most of the advice is on careers, which are mainly interpreted as careers as secretaries, and often as secretaries in just this world: 'the jobs in which a bright girl stands a good chance of getting ahead are usually in Advertising, Public Relations, magazines, newspapers, TV and publishing'; note, in publishing 'secretaries can progress fairly rapidly to assistants and readers'. There are picture guides and written advice on how to behave at an interview, how to prepare for travel as a secretary, and how to acquire knowledge in ways useful in this world: for example, a secretary should be in a position to say to her boss, 'the monsoons tend to make it rather damp in Delhi in August, so don't forget your raincoat'. The impression left is of a magazine teaching partly educated people not just what to consume and how, but which trends in the society to condition themselves to. And at this point we are analysing not so much a *distribution* of interests as their *integration:* basically around advertising, and with a superstructure of the projected values of a public relations world. The older type of woman's magazine can be interestingly compared with these versions of a broadening of horizons.

In magazines for children we find considerable variety, both in content and presentation. An example of the distribution is given in Table 17.

Perhaps the most interesting fact here is the variation between mainly textual and mainly pictorial presentation. It might be thought that those in which pictorial presentation is mainly used are for the youngest children, who are still in an early stage of reading. But these have in fact less pictorial presentation than the straight 'comics', which seem aimed at much older children and which connect directly with comic strips in newspapers. Even in the adventure magazines, for children between about ten and fifteen, the proportion of strip pictorial stories is in most cases high, and seems to be rising. The proportion of school stories is steadily falling; where they still exist, they are of an older,

Table 17

July 1961	Percentage pictorial material	Percentage ordinary text	Editorial features	War	Adventure	Crime	Space	School	Sport	Careers	Comedy	Advertising
Beano	100	0	2	—	37	—	—	—	—	—	61	—
Beezer	100	0	—	—	42	—	—	—	—	—	58	—
Boys' Own	0	100	38	—	26	—	—	—	—	—	3	33
Bunty	81	19	6	—	25	7	—	16	—	37	8	1
Children's Newspaper	39	61	70	—	—	—	—	8	8	—	—	14
Dandy	100	0	—.	12	19	—	—	—	—	—	69	—
Eagle	89	11	29	—.	25	4	8	—	4	—	2	28
Girls' Crystal	81	19	3	—	52	—	—	—	—	20	10	15
Judy	83	17	9	6	46	—	—	—	6	26	5	2
June	80	20	33	—	29	—	—	8	4	15	9	2
Lion	89	11	13	19	17	23	8	8	—	—	2	10
Rover	10	90	—	16	13	10	—	—	51	—	3	7
School Friend	72	28	13	—	29	8	—	8	8	17	10	7
Swift	91	9	16	—	25	9	6	6	3	—	19	16
Tiger	85	15	—	10	20	10	10	—	36	—	5	9
Topper	100	0	—	—	25	—	—	—	—	—	75	—

boarding-school kind. The war stories, where they exist, are given considerable prominence; the combatants are usually British and Nazis. The space-fiction stories seem to be declining in number; almost all are of the 'war of the worlds' type, and though there are very modern and post-modern weapons in them, the conclusive actions are usually fist-fights. The adventure stories are of traditional kinds: sea, exploration, treasure-hunting, jungle, historical (costume), and, above all, cowboys and Indians. The comedy stories are interestingly anarchic, but mainly in quite old-fashioned ways, as if their social world was one or two generations earlier than ours, and still, in certain basic ways, very secure. The standard of drawing and illustration varies considerably, but in almost all cases it is below that in most children's books; in many cases very far below.

We can turn, finally, to look briefly at an important class of magazines, which we usually call weeklies of opinion. Table 18 sets out a sample distribution of space, with the facts about price, size, and circulation.

The distribution between editorial and advertising material follows a general pattern. In *Time and Tide* the low proportion of advertising is probably in relation to circulation, while in *Tribune*, as in the rest of the left-wing Press, both circulation and policy probably keep advertising down. The more established weeklies have always been an important medium for classified notices, but there has recently been a considerable increase in display advertising, especially in the

Table 18 (a)

July 1961	Price in pence	Pages	Average circulation in thousands	Percentage editorial material	Percentage advertising material
Economist	18	116	65	56	44
New Statesman	9	32	85	64	36
Spectator	9	32	48	65	35
Time and Tide	12	40	?	90	10
Tribune	6	12	?	88	12

Table 18 (b)

July 1965	Price in pence	Pages	Average circulation in thousands	Percentage editorial material	Percentage advertising material
Economist	24	92	77	58	42
New Statesman	12	36	89	62	38
Spectator	12	28	37	68	32
Time and Tide	24	52	23	81	19
Tribune	12	16	?	81	19

significant 'inter-company and public opinion' category. Table 19 gives the distribution between classified and display advertising, as percentages of the total space, and also an indication of 'inter-company and public opinion' advertising, again as a percentage of total space.

Table 19 (a)

July 1961	Classified advertisements as a percentage of whole paper	Display advertisements as a percentage of whole paper	Inter-company and public opinion advertising as a percentage of whole paper
Economist	4	40	25
New Statesman	14	22	8
Spectator	5	30	15
Time and Tide	5	5	—
Tribune	2	10	—

Table 19 (b)

July 1965	Classified advertisements as a percentage of whole paper	Display advertisements as a percentage of whole paper	Inter-company and public opinion advertising as a percentage of whole paper
Economist	13	29	25
New Statesman	24	14	10
Spectator	14	18	13
Time and Tide	16	3	0
Tribune	13	6	0

In the later sample, it will be seen that the proportion of display advertising, and with it the inter-company and public opinion proportion to which it is significantly related, has fallen back.

The distribution of editorial space, in these weeklies, is shown in the sample in Table 20.

Table 20 (a)

July 1961	Political and social comment	Arts and books	Financial news and comment	Miscellaneous	Pictures
Economist	40	6	47	7	—
New Statesman	24	37	2	37	—
Spectator	17	31	10	42	—
Time and Tide	13	21	4	36	26
Tribune	53	26	—	17	4

Table 20 (b)

July 1965	Political and social comment	Arts and books	Financial news and comment	Miscellaneous	Pictures
Economist	47	5	42	2	4
New Statesman	39	38	3	20	—
Spectator	42	31	7	18	—
Time and Tide	33	16	16	29	6
Tribune	68	24	0	6	2

Underlying the differences between papers, there is here a characteristic pattern of interests – the minority definitions of arts and politics. The *Economist*'s variations follow the special emphasis of its title, and its high proportion of financial and commercial news and analysis can be compared with the proportions in minority daily and Sunday newspapers. The special political role of *Tribune*, as the organ of a body of opinion unrepresented in the national press, is reflected in its distribution of space. The *New Statesman* and the *Spectator* fluctuate in emphasis; the *Spectator* in particular, under its recent editorship, has become markedly more political in content, and the same trend is evident in the *New Statesman*. However, these emphases are always especially liable to fluctuation. *Time and Tide* has changed substantially in character between the samples. Once a general magazine very similar to the *Spectator* and *New Statesman*, it was in 1961 a much more pictorial magazine, and in 1965 had become a news magazine, apparently following some American models. There is throughout an increasing resemblance between the general weeklies and such newspapers as the *Guardian, Observer* and *Sunday Times*.

It is worth setting the distribution of interests we have seen in various parts of the Press alongside the varying patterns of interest in the two television services. Table 21 (a) shows distribution in a sample week's programmes, reckoned by hours and minutes.

Table 21 (a)

July 1961	News	Documentaries	Discussions	Music (general)	Music (popular)	Panel games	Variety	Religious	Hobbies	Sport	Advertising magazine
BBC	4.40	6.20	2.10	3.00	1.40	0.30	3.40	1.53	0.35	7.50	—
ITV	3.13	2.30	2.20	—	2.05	3.20	3.50	2.30	0.45	3.45	0.45

Table 21 (b)

July 1965	News	Documentary	Music (general)	Music (popular)	Education	Panel games	Variety	Religion	Children	Hobbies	Sport
BBC 1	3.00	8.55	0.50	1.20	0.35	0.25	4.30	2.05	4.30	—	14.00
ITV	3.08	7.30	—	1.10	0.45	0.30	4.45	3.00	5.15	1.10	6.25
BBC2	2.59	5.30	1.35	0.55	1.45	—	1.35	0.30	2.05	0.50	7.20

A further analysis, including BBC 2, is given for continuity in Table 21 (b).* The distribution of drama, by kinds, is given in Table 22.

Table 22 (a)

July 1961	General	Children's	Serials	Films and cartoons	Adventure	Westerns	Crime
BBC	1.45	6.00	0.50	1.50	1.20	4.30	2.45
ITV	4.50	3.55	2.00	3.20	2.30	5.10	7.05

Table 22 (b)

July 1965	General	Children's	Serials	Films and cartoons	Adventure	Westerns	Crime
BBC1	—	1.15	5.25	6.15	0.25	0.50	3.15
ITV	1.00	0.28	8.28	7.35	1.50	0.25	5.20
BBC2	0.15	—	2.55	4.45	—	—	2.15

* The categories in Table 21 (b) have been amended, to include children's programmes, and also education (which is, however, better represented by an autumn week – see Appendix A). The 1961 distinction between documentaries and discussions has become increasingly difficult to maintain, and in the 1965 table these two categories have been merged.

A different type of analysis, designed to show distribution of interests, was undertaken in 1965, for the three television programmes.

Table 23

July 1965	BBC1	ITV	BBC2
FACT	h.m.	h.m.	h.m.
Political, social and economic	8.25	9.43	4.24
Religious	2.05	3.00	0.30
Magazine	2.00	2.25	3.30
Artistic and historical	0.20	0.50	1.25
Scientific	1.10	0.30	1.45
Farming and nature	1.35	1.25	1.20
Sport	14.00	6.25	7.20
Music	2.10	1.10	2.30
Panel games	0.25	1.00	—
Hobbies	1.00	1.45	0.50
Total—FACT	33.10	28.13	23.34
FICTION			
Crime and espionage	3.40	6.10	3.05
Westerns	2.25	0.25	1.15
Domestic	7.05	8.40	0.15
Science	1.15	—	—
Adventure	1.40	4.40	0.25
Comedy	6.05	10.55	3.35
Total—FICTION	22.10	30.50	8.35
Miscellaneous	2.20	—	—
Overall total	57.40	59.03	32.09

Both in 1961 and in 1965, there are less significant differences between the BBC and ITV services than between different parts of the Press. In the 1961 sample, we can note certain differences. There is the much greater share of time given to drama by ITV, in all kinds except plays for children. The greater emphasis on crime plays, on ITV, is particularly marked, while the figures for Westerns, on both channels, are high. There is a larger proportion of panel games on ITV, and a relative absence of orchestral music. The BBC gives more time to sport and to documentary programmes of all kinds.

In the 1965 sample, the two services have in some ways become more like each other, and the new BBC 2 service follows much the same pattern. The BBC's greater emphasis on sport, and its finding of time for orchestral music, are still evident. On the other hand, ITV has decreased its panel games and increased its documentary programmes, where in quantity it is not now much inferior to the BBC. ITV still gives more time to drama, but on both services there has been a marked increase of time given to films (usually old commercial productions bought cheaply from the United States, which is also a source for many serials). In time given to crime and espionage plays, the difference between the channels is still evident, but it is worth noting that the overall content of this kind of work has increased. On each channel, meanwhile, there are less television Westerns, though these are still heavily represented among the old films. The most striking development in the field of drama is the increase in the number of serials, many of which are in effect package programming. It is worth adding that as well as the increasing similarity between BBC and ITV, there is a good deal of evidence of deliberate matching, of a competitive kind, on the two major channels. A good deal of programme planning is evidently done with an eye to the other channel, rather than by any more general criterion.

73

Finally, it is worth comparing the proportions of time given to political, social and economic programmes, out of all material televised. The figure for BBC 1 is fifteen per cent, for ITV sixteen and a half per cent, and for BBC 2 fourteen per cent. These proportions are closely comparable with those for popular daily newspapers.

There are more emphatic differences in the distribution of interests in the various BBC sound programmes. Table 24 sets out a sample week's distribution.

Table 24 (a)

July 1961	Home	Light	Third	Network Three
	h.m	h.m	h.m	h.m
News	15.50	6.25	—	—
Magazine	10.35	6.30	—	—
Documentary	4.50	2.10	1.00	—
Discussion	7.30	1.00	2.40	1.30
General Talks	5.35	0.30	3.30	0.50
General Readings	2.40	1.50	—	—
Poetry	—	—	1.35	—
Music (general)	30.20	7.25	9.50	1.00
Music (popular)	7.30	71.20	—	—
Opera	1.30	—	4.50	—
Drama (classic)	—	—	0.35	—
Drama (general modern)	2.30	1.30	1.30	—
Drama (serials)	—	4.45	—	—
Drama (adventure)	3.05	0.30	—	—
Drama (crime)	2.00	1.00	—	—
Children	2.10	1.55	—	—
Hobbies	0.30	—	—	1.15
Languages	—	—	—	—
Sport	2.50	6.10	—	*
Variety	2.30	9.30	—	—
Panel games	2.00	1.00	—	—

Table 24 (b)

July 1965	Home	Light	Third	Network Three
News	18.30	4.00	1.10	1.32
Religion	6.45	0.25	0.20	—
Magazine	26.35	—	—	—
Documentary	3.15	—	2.00	—
Discussion	3.15	1.30	2.25	—
General Talks	4.03	—	2.40	—
General Readings	4.00	1.15	—	—
Poetry	—	—	1.35	—
Music (general)	13.00	—	13.10	52.30
Music (popular)	9.05	114.40	—	1.30
Opera	—	—	1.55	0.30
Drama (classic)	—	—	1.00	—
Drama (general modern)	6.45	2.10	2.10	—
Drama (serials)	4.45	4.00	—	—
Drama (adventure)	0.30	1.00	—	—
Drama (crime)	0.30	—	—	—
Children	3.35	—	—	—
Education (+languages)	1.30	—	—	5.00
Hobbies	2.30	—	—	—
Sport	1.48	1.50	—	19.15*
Variety	1.30	5.30	—	—
Panel Games	3.40	1.10	—	—

*The Test Match ball-by-ball commentary (more than six hours on each day of play) was broadcast on this wavelength.

It used to be said that the BBC sound programmes formed a pyramid of separate levels of taste and interest and seriousness, on which listeners might move from the base of the Light through the middle levels of the Home to the apex of the Third. This is not now BBC policy, which has been defined as the provision of planned alternative listening. It is clear that the latter emphasis has become much more marked between 1961 and 1965. The figures for music programmes are the most evident result of thinking in terms of separate levels of taste, and this trend has gone much further in the 1965 figures, within a general expansion of music broadcasting. In the same way, the complex of news, magazine, documentary and discussion programmes, represented in 1961 by a proportion of $3\frac{1}{2}$ Home to 1 Light, is now a proportion of 9 Home to 1 Light. To the extent that there is still an evident mutual connection between the programmes, the policy can be described as planned alternative listening, but it is true to say also that a marked degree of cultural specialization, very similar to that in the Press, is increasingly apparent.

ANALYSIS

From measurement by categories we can see something of the distribution of interests in various kinds of paper and programme. Yet to see the full body of what is communicated we have to look at the varying ways in which these interests are presented.

Headlines

We can learn a good deal about the tone and interest of particular newspapers simply by comparing head-lines. Here is a sample of main headlines from an average week in 1961:

MONDAY

Times	RUSSIA DISPLAYS HER AIR POWER
Guardian	RUSSIA SHOWS OFF HER AIR POWER
Telegraph	RUSSIA DISPLAYS HER MISSILES
Mail	MR K'S SKY-OPENER
Express	KRUSCHEV SHOWS OFF
Herald	THE MIGHTIEST OF ALL AIR SHOWS – BY MR K
Worker	PRICE-RISE, PAY-PEG PLAN

CONTENT

Mirror	CRUTCHES FOR THE DUKE
Sketch	ROPED CHILD FOUND IN LAKE

TUESDAY

Times	MR KENNEDY ORDERS DEFENCE REVIEW
Guardian	MR KENNEDY ORDERS DEFENCE REVIEW
Telegraph	MENZIES CLASH ON COMMON MARKET
Mail	SIX SAY: LET'S TALK
Express	SANDYS C AND B MENZIES O
Herald	THE SIX CALL BRITAIN TO TALKS ON AUGUST 1
Worker	WELCOME SPACEMAN!
Mirror	STUFFED SHIRTS IN THE SPACE AGE
Sketch	RAF BOFFIN WILL QUIZ GAGA

WEDNESDAY

Times	CHEERING CROWDS HAIL MAJOR GAGARIN
Guardian	HERO'S WELCOME FOR MAJOR GAGARIN
Telegraph	GAGARIN LUNCH WITH QUEEN
Mail	SHAKE! 2,000 TIMES
Express	FANTASTICHESKY
Herald	LONDON GIVES LITTLE YURI THE BIG HAND
Worker	A REAL HERO'S WELCOME
Mirror	RADY VAS VIDJETJI
Sketch	GA-GA OVER GAGA

THURSDAY

Times	US MISSILE DETECTOR LAUNCHED
Guardian	MISSILE TRACKER IN ORBIT
Telegraph	COMMANDOS WILL QUIT KUWAIT
Mail	PREMIER TO WARN
Express	RED EXPERTS PERISH
Herald	US PUTS 'SPY IN THE SKY' OVER RUSSIA
Worker	PANZERS HERE IN AUTUMN
Mirror	THE GIRL WHO GAVE YURI A KISS
Sketch	1-TON WHALE AMOK AT KEW

COMMUNICATIONS

FRIDAY

Times	EMERGENCY ACTION TO RESTORE ECONOMY
Guardian	SHIPYARDS INQUIRY BY GOVERNMENT
Telegraph	PREMIER ANXIOUS BUT 'NO FEARS'
Mail	MAC PLAYS IT CALM
Express	WORRIED — NOT AFRAID
Herald	I'M WORRIED BUT NOT AFRAID, SAYS PREMIER
Worker	BAN-BOMB: SMASHING VICTORY
Mirror	BURIED ALIVE!
Sketch	THIS IS MY AXE

SATURDAY

Times	GEN. KASSEM RENEWS CLAIM TO KUWAIT
Guardian	•FBI MISGIVINGS ON COMMON MARKET
Telegraph	TUC TO MEET ON ETU CRISIS
Mail	STRIKE HALTS BOAC
Express	STRIKE STOPS PLANES
Herald	THE CRISIS: TORIES NOW TURN TO PLANNING
Worker	MAC PLANS A WAGE CUT IN DISGUISE
Mirror	TUC PROBE SHOCK FOR RED UNION
Sketch	BOAC STRUCK DEAD

These may be compared with further examples. Here is a sample of Sunday newspaper headlines (July, 1965):

SUNDAY

Times	US WANTS TO SEAL OFF N VIETNAM AND EXTEND BOMBING
Observer	CALLAGHAN PUTTING US IN PAWN — LLOYD
Telegraph	HEATH DAMAGED BY COUP THAT COLLAPSED — CLUMSY INTRIGUE
Express	NEW RAIL THREAT AS GO-SLOW SPREADS
People	LOUSIEST SUMMER IN YEARS!
News of the World	WHY I ESCAPED — BY BIGGS
Citizen	WILSON SLAMS WORK-TO-RULE
Mirror	IT'S HEARTBREAK AT THE FORUM

CONTENT

We have become used to this familiar range of emphasis within the British Press. It is worth comparing the newspaper headlines of two sample days with the headlines of the BBC morning news bulletins:

MONDAY, 5 JULY, 1965

BBC   Extra police were sent to the American Embassy in London last night after a home-made bomb had exploded at the West End Office of the American Express Company.

At least twelve people were killed and hundreds injured when a whirlwind swept across Northern Italy.

American bombers, based on Guam Island, have again attacked Vietcong guerillas in South Vietnam.

The Transport and General Workers conference begins today. The Acting General-Secretary says he thinks delegates will reject the Government's Incomes Policy.

A cloudy day, with sunny intervals, is forecast for all districts.

Times	US BANS ATTACKS ON MISSILE SITES
Guardian	MR GRIMOND WARNS OF DANGER TO WEST
Telegraph	BOMB AT LONDON US AGENCY
Mail	INSIDE SOUTH AFRICA'S GAOLS
Express	BOMB BLAST DRAMA
Sun	MR EXPORTS SHOWS HOW
Worker	BELT UP – STICK TO POLO
Mirror	PEER JOINS ROW OVER THE DUKE
Sketch	MP'S CLASH OVER PHILIP

SATURDAY, 10 JULY, 1965

BBC   A man in West London has given the police information about the furniture van used in the Wandsworth Jail break.

In Washington, the House of Representatives has passed the Bill to give Negroes the vote unconditionally.

79

General Franco's new Cabinet has promised a more representative political set-up for Spain.
Queen Anne-Marie of Greece has given birth to a daughter.
North Vietnam has ruled out any question of meeting the Commonwealth peace mission.
Some Labour backbench MPs are campaigning this weekend over the issue of Parliamentary privilege.
A mainly dry day is forecast, although there's a chance of rain spreading into western areas later.

Times	HANOI REJECTION OF BRITISH OVERTURE
Guardian	LBJ FORECASTS WORSENING OF VIETNAM WAR
Telegraph	COUNTRY HOUSE HUNT FOR BIGGS
Mail	I PAINTED THE ESCAPE VAN
Express	SHOTGUN DRAGNET
Sun	BIGGS TEAR-GAS SIEGE
Worker	JOHNSON'S VIETNAM THREAT
Mirror	150 POLICE RAID MANSION — BUT NO BIGGS
Sketch	CLUE OF THE RED VAN — MAN TALKS TO YARD

The selection of its main story, by each newspaper, can be compared with the selection of items by the BBC. The order of priority within the BBC bulletins also deserves scrutiny. (Note: it should be remembered that there is some difference in times of news becoming available, between the papers and the broadcast bulletins. The main differences, however, seem little related to this fact, in these examples.)

One further kind of comparison can be made, between headlines indicating main news stories in British and other newspapers on a particular day. The following examples come from 7 and 8 December, 1965, in the British morning papers and in a random selection of newspapers in other countries:

81

	COMRADES IN THE PARTY AND COUNTRY URGE MAKING GOOD BROADCASTS TO SERVE THE PEOPLE OF CHINA AND THE WHOLE WORLD
Times	TWO GOVERNMENT VOICES ON MR SMITH
Guardian	MR BOTTOMLEY CALLS MR SMITH A LIAR
Telegraph	SMITH LIED, SAYS BOTTOMLEY
Mail	CHRISTMAS EVE BUS THREAT
Express	MOORS: 'DEATH BOASTS' DRAMA
Sun	STOP OIL SHIP, DEMAND MPS
Worker	'STOP OIL FOR SMITH'
Mirror	MOOR COURT TOLD OF MURDER BY AXE
Sketch	COUPLE JOKED AFTER MURDER WITH AXE

* Issue of 9 December, as nearest available.

Presenting a story

The briefest comparison of headlines shows obvious variations in the story considered most important, in its presentation or angling, and in language and tone. It is worth following these aspects through the presentation of one story, from the same week's papers.

The story chosen is the debate and vote on foreign policy and defence at the 1961 conference of the Transport and General Workers' Union. There had been considerable advance commentary and speculation on the result of this debate, but the actual result was given first place in the day's news by only one paper, the *Worker*, which alone has an editorial policy close to the policy supported by the conference. It is fair to assume that if the vote had gone the other way, this situation would have been reversed.

The Times gave the report 23 c.i. (column inches) on a subsidiary news page; the *Guardian* 22 c.i. in the lower middle of the front page; the *Telegraph* $11\frac{7}{8}$ c.i. on front and back pages, and $34\frac{1}{2}$ c.i. on a back inside page; the *Mail* 23 c.i. on an inside page; the *Express* 28 c.i. on the front page; the *Herald* $\frac{3}{4}$ c.i. on the front page and $62\frac{1}{4}$ c.i. on a back inside page; the *Worker* 30 c.i. in a front page lead story; the *Mirror* $23\frac{1}{4}$ c.i. on an inside page; the *Sketch* $13\frac{1}{4}$ c.i. on an inside page.

In all headlines, except those of the BBC Home Service News and the *Worker*, the issue was personalized in Mr Cousins, the General Secretary. The BBC headline was: 'The Transport Union has reaffirmed its Ban the Bomb policy by a 4 to 1 vote'. The *Worker* headline was: 'Ban-Bomb: Smashing Victory'. Other headlines were: *The Times:* 'Mr Cousins Wins Fight to keep Unilateralism'; *Guardian:* 'Mr Cousins holds Transport Union to Unilateralism'; *Telegraph:* 'Mr Cousins's majority shrinks'; *Mail:* 'Cousins triumphs over Bomb Vote'; *Express:* 'The Winner – Battling Cousins'; *Herald:* 'Cousins Wins by 3 to 1' and on its front page 'The Odd-One-Out'; *Mirror:* 'H-Bomb Victory for Cousins'; *Sketch:* 'Cousins Wins Bomb Battle'.

On this issue, there can be legitimate differences of political interpretation, but reduction to this extreme kind of personalization is in fact a familiar method of angling news. The use of phrases like 'bomb battle' and 'battling Cousins', and in subsidiary headlines 'bomb bout', 'rebel line', 'bomb vote', is also in effect prejudicial. The same is true of the *Worker*'s 'smashing victory'. In the *Express* this effect is underlined by a cartoon showing Mr Cousins as a boxer, with his foot on the chest of Mr Gaitskell. A different effect is achieved by the *Herald*'s use of 'the odd-one-out'. All these devices are familiar ways of inserting a political or emotional interpretation of the news into its actual reporting. A response to the news is powerfully suggested, either before the news is given or in the course of giving it.

The point about personalization has to be assessed from the actual report of speakers in the debate. *The Times* report gives fifty-two speakers for the successful motion, and thirty-five for an alternative motion, with one 'undecided'. These figures are repeated in the *Guardian, Telegraph, Herald, Mail, Mirror;* the *Express* gives fifty-two and thirty-five. The *Worker* gives no figures, and no breakdown. The *Sketch* gives 'more than eighty', and the BBC gave 'nearly a hundred'. In all reports but that in *The Times*, the groups of speakers are interpreted: as 'unilateralists' and 'multilateralists' in the *Guardian;* as 'unilateralists' and 'Gaitskell supporters' in the *Telegraph;* as 'for unilateralism' and 'for collective disarmament' in the *Mail;* as 'for Cousins' and 'for multilateral disarmament' in the *Express;* as 'for Cousins' and 'against' in the *Herald;* as 'for' and 'against' in the *Mirror*. The *Telegraph* interpretation has to be set against *The Times* report that Mr Gaitskell 'came in for abuse from both sides'. Only the *Telegraph* reports the actual terms of the successful motion, and although the issue had been widely discussed beforehand it is probable that many readers of the other papers would be to some extent uncertain about the exact policy being debated.

Reports of the length of the debate, where given, varied from 'all day' (BBC) and 'day-long' (*Worker*) to 6 hours (*Mail, Express, Mirror*), 5½ hours (*Herald*), and 5 hours (*Times*). Reports of the majority for the successful motion included '4 to 1' (BBC, quoting its Industrial Correspondent's estimate), '4 to 1' (*Mail*). 'between 3 and 4 to 1' (*Mirror*), 'about 590 to 170' (*Telegraph*), '3 to 1' (*Times, Express, Sketch*). The *Guardian* quoted varying estimates of the show of hands, from '5 or 6 to 1' to 'more like 5 to 2', and gave a 'consensus of opinion among a group of reporters' as '3 to 1', while noting that in the circumstances all estimating was 'hazardous'. The *Herald* said that 'some estimates put today's majority even higher than 3 to 1'. It added that of the 769 delegates there were 'at most' 150 hands against. The *Telegraph* reported that it 'appeared to most observers' that '170 showed their opposition to the General Secretary', though estimates of the minority varied between 100 and 200. The *Express* reported '180 against him'. The *Worker* reported the minority as 'less than a tenth'.

Interpretations of the result ranged from 'tremendous personal triumph' (*Mail*), 'striking personal triumph' (*Mirror*), 'his most significant victory' (*Herald*) to the *Telegraph*'s 'the result can be fairly regarded as an achievement for both sides'. Comparisons with the vote of the previous conference ranged from 'majority severely reduced' (*Guardian*), 'majority shrinks' (*Telegraph*), 'far smaller than at last conference' (*Sketch*), to the *Herald*'s comment that at the last conference the majority was '14 to 1', 'but that was in a different context'.

Reports of the actual speeches varied in emphasis. *The Times* reported the proposer and seconder of the successful motion in 3 c.i. and the proposer and seconder of the unsuccessful motion in 4 c.i. It added $\frac{3}{4}$ c.i. and $1\frac{1}{8}$ c.i. general summary respectively. Mr Cousins's speech was reported in $3\frac{1}{4}$ c.i. This balance, 7 c.i. for fifty-two speakers, $5\frac{1}{8}$ for thirty-five speakers, came through elsewhere as: *Guardian*, $7\frac{1}{8}$ and $1\frac{3}{8}$; *Telegraph*, $15\frac{1}{2}$ and $2\frac{1}{4}$; *Mail*, 3 and $2\frac{1}{2}$; *Express*, $1\frac{5}{8}$ and nil; *Herald* $7\frac{7}{8}$ and $6\frac{1}{8}$; *Worker* $11\frac{1}{4}$ and nil; *Mirror* $3\frac{1}{4}$ and nil; *Sketch*, $\frac{1}{2}$ and $2\frac{7}{8}$. The largest item in all these reports was the speech of Mr Cousins, except in the *Sketch*.

In the reporting of speeches *The Times* made little comment. The *Guardian* described Mr Cousins as 'like an avenging angel' and his speech as 'powerful if confusing'. The *Telegraph* described Mr Cousins as 'at his most messianic', The *Mail* reported that he 'thundered passionately'. The *Express* reported 'his tornado of a speech', described it as 'noteworthy as much for its arrogant self-assurance as for its eloquent sincerity', and introduced its limited direct quotation with 'he roared'. The *Herald* reported a 'dramatic speech'. The *Worker* made no comment. The *Mirror* reported 'one of the most powerful speeches of his career' and described thirty-eight minutes of 'impassioned words'. The *Sketch* reported that Mr Cousins 'spoke passionately – in his shirt sleeves'.

'*Sex*' in the Sunday papers

It has become commonplace to complain that there is too much 'sex' in certain Sunday papers, but it is necessary to analyse this content further. In general, there is a fairly regular association of sex with crime, and a subsidiary association of sex with professional entertainment, particularly with pictures of actresses and models. These associations would seem to determine what is normally meant, in these papers, by 'sex'. Other kinds of report are rare.

Apart from the photographs of actresses and models, and reports of the reputed affairs of film stars and similar personalities, there seem to be two main categories. The papers concerned are principally the *News of the World* and (in 1961) the *People* and the *Pictorial*. The first category is the reporting of court cases involving adultery, seduction, rape, homosexuality, indecent exposure, and prostitution. The *News of the World* seems to specialize in this kind of report;

other papers take up only certain spectacular cases. The reporting is usually quite straight, though the headlines are angled: 'When Her Husband had to Whistle'; 'At 2 a.m. After a Dance was Over'; '18 Photos in her Dressing-Table Drawer'. Sometimes a case is written up, by a named reporter: 'A Den of Vice in an Old Country Town'.

A second category derives from fact, or alleged fact, but not as regular reporting. One group in this category is that of 'memoirs' or 'confessions', either of persons involved in prosecution or scandal, or of persons prominent in entertainment. These works are advertised and headlined in such ways as 'My Wicked Life' or 'I Was Tempted and I Fell', and it is sometimes implied that they should be read as a warning. The same implication of moral warning, or of a necessary exposure of unpleasant facts, is usually given to another group in this category: 'investigations' undertaken by the newspaper itself. An example is 'The Amazing Double Life of X.Y.' (name and photograph printed) – 'infant teacher and call-girl', advertised as 'by the *People* investigators'. Two reporters, 'acting on information already gathered', made contact with this woman, without disclosing themselves as reporters, to try to prove her "activities as a prostitute". A different kind of independent investigation is the report on some place or habit, as in the same issue of the *People*: ' "Love-drug" is killing half a million', a report by an independent writer on prostitution and heroin-addiction in the harbour area of Hong Kong. Of this article the paper says: 'It may shock you. But it must be told.'

Some patterns of fiction in women's magazines

Seventy stories, from twenty-two women's magazines, have been read and analysed. The most striking general feature of most of the stories is that they were evidently written to promote a particular psychological process in the reader. The literary skills used are subordinate to this intention. None has any independent literary intentions or merits.

There is an interesting difference between the normal setting of short stories and of serials: the former are usually set in the home, the latter in some 'exotic' environment (Paris, an Australian sheep farm, Iraq). Of forty stories set in the home, thirty-nine are in middle-class homes; the exception is in one of the very cheap fiction magazines. Where stories are set in a place of work, the typical places are offices, hospitals, airports and ocean liners, the countryside. The whole ordinary range of industrial and shop work is only very occasionally touched.

The social status of the hero is usually a point of interest in the story. Of sixty-nine heroes, only two are described without reference to standing at work. Of the other sixty-seven, two are foreign aristocrats, sixty-four are in 'middle-class' jobs, mainly the professions, and are described as successful in them, while one hero was poor but returns successful from Australia. Almost invariably the social standing of the hero, in these terms, is higher than that of the heroine, and the typical engagement or marriage is 'upwards' in this sense. Marrying 'the boss' is quite regular. The ordinary sign of the hero's success is his car, which is often made a point of emotional interest.

The plots of the stories show certain regular patterns. Twenty-seven of the seventy are a familiar kind of intrigue fiction, often in exotic settings, with crises due to misunderstandings and secrets, and most of the scenes set at balls, weddings, and parties. Three others are in effect anecdotes, humorous or ironic in tone, by male authors. The other forty are concerned with the solution of certain typical emotional difficulties. In these, three methods stand out. Seven stories are in intention therapeutic. A situation such as fear of love, or despair at being jilted or deceived, is taken from the point of view of the heroine. The solution here is always adjustment: a child, an animal, a place overcomes the fear of love; the deceived wife adjusts invariably towards husband, children, and home. The emotional tone of these stories is very similar to that of the practical advice columns, which normally advise adjustment to a difficult situation rather than an attempt to change it.

The other thirty-three stories have solutions in wish-fulfilment (fourteen), or in a kind of magical extraction of the difficulty (nineteen). In the former, the plain, unsuccessful, shy, or jilted girl gets the best (most prosperous) husband in the end. The stories are written from her point of view, and the reader is evidently invited to identify with her. In contrast with these stories, where it all somehow (though for no evident reason) comes right in the end, the 'extraction' stories centre on scenes of critical revelation: the rival is shown up in her true (bad) colours and is overcome, or the jealousy was never really necessary (he had never loved the other anyway, in spite of all appearances to the contrary). The world adjusts to the heroine, not by any action on her part, but by a sudden extraction of the painful element. In the wish-fulfilment stories it just quietly adjusts.

Thus, not only are most women's homes and jobs, and most kinds of men, excluded from these stories, but also any kind of persistent problem and any permanently difficult relationship.

Style in advertising

The basic method of commercial advertising has always been exaggeration, from the seventeenth-century notice of a dentrifice which would not only clean the teeth but fix them and prevent them dropping out, to the contemporary advertisement, in a magazine for Africans, of a preparation that will 'cream your skin lighter'. In the search for superlatives, the limits of sense have long been passed ('whiter than white'), and for a generation the natural reaction to this has been capitalized, in humorous exaggeration ('Guinness – Him Strong'), even while the superlatives continue.

There is still some plain recommendation of products, but the more usual method is to associate the product with some other desirable thing: health, love, respect. This kind of association can be almost infinitely graded: from the strip-cartoon, in an African magazine, recommending a kitchen soap as the way to bring friends home (otherwise the curtains are 'all in holes' and you are ashamed), to the full-colour page, in an English magazine, showing a woman in a mink stole, in a fashionable street filled with long expensive cars, with a chauffeur behind her carrying a long expensive sink. ('So Henry said . . . go out and buy one. So I did . . . Simply acres of draining-board. Such a blissful sink.')

But there is another kind of grading, more subtle in its operation. There is the direct promise of a husband or a better job if a particular product, which can be almost anything, is used, and the reaction against this is again exploited, by repeating the claim with humorous exaggeration. Then there is the indirect promise of the same kind, ranging from a simple side-by-side layout of the product and a desirable situation, to the creation of an atmosphere of dream and dreaminess (often by blurred photography and a use of deep colours).

From one week's newspapers, I have in front of me three pictures of yachting, all of which might have been taken at the same time. Each picture occupies three-quarters of the space of the advertisement, and the name of the product is in each case unobtrusive. It is only by inspection that we find them advertising, respectively, bread, a fruit squash, and a bank. From a magazine in the same week, there is a picture of a cool girl in blue surrounded by six men in black and red, all looking up at her from the darkness. This is 'a fabulous feeling that we call "Colour Confidence" ': the product is a make-up, and 'pressmen of the world applaud'.

The common appearance of advertisements of this kind, though only a development from the simpler kind in which a packet of pills was placed alongside a drawing of a doctor or nurse, is now very important. In a sense, the product has become irrelevant: the advertiser is working directly on images and dreams. The concentration of such advertisements creates a whole style of life, centred largely in fantasy, which is in effect a common interest of all advertisers rather than the recommendation of particular products. All ordinary values are temporarily over-ridden by a kind of bastard art, not clarifying experience but deliberately confusing it.

It is then no surprise, in a half-page of our most serious newspaper, to find, beside a pleasant picture, these words: 'crust of concrete: push of polyanthus. Polyanthus breaks through . . . naturally', and then 'the week-end is the most natural break of all'. This is a recommendation of television advertising, in those controversial 'natural breaks'. It is completed by the small-type promise: 'at the week-end your commercials penetrate deeply'. We can probably agree that this is what it is all about.

SURVEY

Two facts stand out, when we survey the general field of communications in contemporary Britain. These are, first, the increasingly close connexion between the methods and content of advertising and editorial material, and, second, the marked division of material into classes, which then normally keep to their own world.

The connexion with advertising is of several kinds. The most important is in fact quite difficult to see, unless historical comparisons are introduced. This is the increasing visual similarity of newspapers and advertisements, in typography, layout, and photographic style. Newspapers like *The Times*, which are still quite traditional in layout, show this most clearly by contrast: the regular columns of close print, with small-type headlines, are very different from the sudden large headlines, broken-column layout, and the combination of words and photographs, in a single effect, of the advertisements. The paper's general photographs are separate from printed news, while its news photographs have usually an immediate relevance to the report. Most advertisement photographs have no direct relevance to the product, or combine some other interest with the product. In the popular newspapers many of the photographs are of this kind, making a direct and often isolated visual appeal. It is difficult, in the popular papers, to separate, at first glance, the news and advertisement photographs, while in layout and typography there is often no distinction between advertising and editorial material. It is then not possible to separate advertising from the general effect of the paper. It is not an isolated item, a kind of support cost, but part of the total communication. The most extreme development of this kind is in the women's magazines, where it is often difficult, without close inspection, to identify an advertisement, and where the verbal and visual styles combine with the similarity of interest to produce a single overall effect. Another relevant case is the advertising supplement, in which apparently independent editorial treatment of products and services is printed alongside direct advertisement, in a planned way.

Historically, the magazine followed the book in style, while the daily newspaper expanded the magazine. The early Sunday newspapers followed printed ballads and broadsheets, with one or two large headlines, and a main illustration, followed by close print. In most newspapers and magazines the style is now that of the advertisement: it was in posters and display advertisements that the use of varied type-sizes, of slogans, and of the planned combination of visual and verbal effect, developed. A neutral look at a two-page spread of a popular newspaper gives the effect of a jig-saw of posters, display advertisements, and display stories. The direction of emotional interest and response by advertising slogans is now directly paralleled in popular newspapers and headlines. In the list of headlines, those from the more traditional papers were consistently easier to understand, as a summary of the main news. Many of the others did not even attempt this, but caught interest, and included emotional reaction, in ways very familiar from general advertising. (Compare the uses of 'axe' and 'dead' in the 1961 *Sketch* headlines, to describe, respectively, economic proposals and grounded aircraft.) Whole pages, planned around headlines of this kind, and around photographs, seem to be aiming to make a single overall emotional effect. Thus a style of communication, developed for the selling of products, has to a considerable extent taken over the presentation of news and opinion.

There is also a connexion with advertising in the second general fact: the division of material into classes. Any reasonable survey of the whole content of contemporary communications shows few omissions. Almost any interest and any level of attention is in fact provided for. There are of course striking cases of particular proportions of interest, as in crime and accidents. But most people, choosing from the whole range, could get what they want. Within this general coverage, however, there are quite rigid divisions, and these seem to be increasing.

In magazines and in broadcasting there has been a marked tendency, since the war, to split up general material into particular interests and tastes, rather than covering a general field in a single magazine or service. The old general-interest magazines have mostly gone, to be replaced by special-interest magazines for particular classes of user. The division of broadcasting into Light, Home, and Third programmes has had the same fragmenting effect. In television a general programme is still offered, but within this there is a characteristic specialization in relation to hours of viewing: the peak hours, for obvious reasons, carrying programmes of known popular appeal, while new or minority programmes (even for very sizeable minorities) tend to be put into off-peak periods. This is often regrettable, but it is still in many ways better than the division into separate kinds of service which is normal elsewhere.

To many people the development of separate classes of newspaper, magazine and broadcast programme seems natural. In certain cases, of course, the development of specialized media is a sign of cultural growth, which often brings a useful and necessary specialization. This is not, however, in the general field of public communications, the only trend. Two other kinds of pressure are also evident: the pressure of advertisers to have magazines with particular classes of readers who will provide a known market; and the influence of a conventional class-model of British society, divided into upper, middle, and lower groups. The original model of secondary education also assumed three groups, but these are steadily being reduced to two, and there are signs of a similar development in the Press, which now divides much more easily into 'quality' and 'popular', with the steady disappearance of 'middle' papers, than it did a generation ago.

The result is not only that certain interests tend to become specialized to and identified with particular social classes (as, most obviously, serious politics and the traditional arts with the minority). It is also that opportunities for movement between these groups, and for variation of interest within individuals and families, have now to be quite consciously sought. You change your newspaper or magazine, or switch to another service, to make this change of interest. Since individuals and families are in fact very variable, over the whole field, and while classifiable in groups are not as rigidly separate from each other as the differences between newspapers, magazines, and programmes would suggest, this increasing typification is a very serious social tendency. It is worth noting that it is also used, both as a means of social classification ('top people', 'a Third Programme type', 'the average reader of the *Daily Mirror*'), and as a way of recommending papers and magazines, as in general advertising ('discriminating people smoke x; top people read y'). Meanwhile the evidence of ordinary social and educational investigations reveals no such rigid divisions, but gradual scales of many kinds, which, while reflected in the total content of communications, are not reflected in actual distribution.

There are many genuine problems of communication in a large society which is almost wholly literate yet which has deep educational and social differences. Looking through the material, we see an obvious use of formulas – about a type of reader or listener, and then about his interests and styles and tones. The minority newspapers and magazines can be as rigid in this kind of assumption as the popular productions. Since communication of any kind depends on an element of convention, these formulas can become quite deeply learned, and any growth or change beyond them can be very difficult. We all get used to particular styles and layouts, which have no necessary relevance to the real interests and material, but which we might feel lost without. In actual content and presentation, now, the formulas seem to be hardening: 'the masses' – crime, sex, sport, personalities, entertainment, pictures; 'the minority' – traditional politics, traditional arts, briefings on popular trends. It is then a matter for argument whether 'the masses' and 'the minority' are inevitable social facts, or whether they are communication models which in part create and reinforce the situation they apparently describe.

4
Controversy

THE MASSES

SURELY we get the culture we deserve. Most things that we produce have to be sold, or they will not go on being produced. Does not this mean, then, that what people are now actually buying is what they want?

Of course [Mr Cecil King, head of the *Mirror* group, said recently] you have got to give the public what it wants, otherwise you go out of business as we have seen recently in the case of two or three newspapers. You try and raise its standards as well. The trouble is the critics imagine the great British public is as educated as themselves and their friends, and that we ought to start where they are and raise the standard from there up. In point of fact it is only the people who conduct newspapers and similar organizations who have any idea quite how indifferent, quite how stupid, quite how uninterested in education of any kind the great bulk of the British public are.

Mr Norman Collins, of Independent Television, added:

If one gave the public exactly what it wanted it would be a perfectly appalling service. . . . It is quite obvious that the educational standard of this country is deplorable. . . . The overwhelming mass of the letters we get are illiterate, they are ungrammatical, they are deplorably written, and what is more distressing, too, they evince an attitude of mind that I do not think can be regarded as very admirable. All they write for are pictures of film stars, television stars, or asking why there are not more jazz programmes, why there cannot be more programmes of a music-hall type. I hold the teachers very largely responsible, if that is the attitude of people in their teens and early twenties. If we provided simply that it would be deplorable.

97

Now clearly Mr King and Mr Collins know a lot about public taste. Ought we not simply to accept their conclusions? The masses are stupid and indifferent; we do our best for them, within those limits. The traditional idea of a people wanting light, of democracy as a way of spreading the light, is perhaps merely sentimental. The reality shows otherwise.

But does it, in quite this way? Mr King and Mr Collins are practitioners, and their evidence is consistent. But another kind of evidence comes from research workers and teachers. Mr Joseph Trenaman, Granada Research Fellow, University of Leeds, has said:

It is sometimes said that the bulk of the population do not want to learn, they only want to be entertained. This view has no foundation in fact whatsoever. I know of no research or other evidence to support such a view, whereas there is evidence to the contrary. . . . Partly the difficulty is that for less educated people the responses to knowledge are connected with their attitudes to social and class differences, and the plain fact is that what we loosely call culture is identified in their minds with status, with rewards and with power in our society.

Mr Jack Longland, Director of Education for Derbyshire, has said:

Most of these opportunities now for the first time offered by Press and broadcasting, cheap reading, cinema and advertising will continue to be lost if you go on underestimating the intelligence, capacities, tastes and interests of your new mass public. We who are in the business of education have compelling reasons for knowing that this is true. You see, we have met all the members of your future mass-communications society already and have got to know them pretty well.

Mr Longland went on to give examples of the range of creative and voluntary educational activities which most children find excitement and satisfaction in, only to be exposed to 'the full blare of the world of mass communications after school life is over'.

What interests me, in these statements, is the real conflict of evidence. These men are speaking honestly from their experience, in what seems a common field, and reaching quite opposite conclusions. Why?

First, I think, because in fact they are looking at different things. Mr King and Mr Collins are looking at evidence in direct relation to their own existing services, and of course this evidence is powerful. Mr Trenaman and Mr Longland are looking at evidence of a different kind, in other situations and institutions, and in part they are looking at potential interest, which in many ways, and for differing reasons, fails to develop adequately with things as they are. These two kinds of evidence must always be remembered. It is very easy to think of the cultural level of a people as something single and something fixed. This is the trouble with phrases like 'the masses' and 'the great British public', which lead us to think not of actual people, living and growing in different ways, but of some large many-headed thing with fixed habits. For the people Mr Trenaman was talking about, there might be no registered evidence of actual participation in 'what we loosely call culture', while this goes on being identified with 'social and class differences'. But this identification is a product of history, and could change. For the children Mr Longland was talking about, there is a critical passage from being a child to being an adult, and since for most of them the age of leaving school is about the age of becoming physically mature, they could not in any case go on with the same interests in quite the same way. But if the world of active education is identified with childhood, while the world of 'mass communications' is identified with the greater freedom of the adult, the personal choice is very difficult. Once again, however, this identification is a product of history, and could change. It is by no means necessary that the majority school-leaving age should coincide with the age of puberty, thus often encouraging the idea that education is one of the childish things you put away.

Growth and change are central to this whole problem. But if you have a fixed idea about 'the masses', you cannot really take them into account. There is evidence that by taking an aspect of public taste, at a given time, and giving great publicity to it, you can make it more fixed, more emphatic, more important than it originally was. Dr Hilde Himmelweit, who directed the research published as *Television and the Child*, had this to say from the evidence of comparative studies over a period:

It is liked, therefore its rating is high, therefore it is put on at peak viewing hours; and so the vicious circle is set up. I think one could very easily argue if one only looked at today's ratings – what can you expect? After all, people like Westerns, we put Westerns on. But because we have this trend study extending over a period of five years you can see that this kind of taste is to some extent – not of course entirely – an artificial one, a taste produced by the programme planners and producers.

It seems to be generally agreed that in the movement of public taste and opinion you cannot start a trend but you can accentuate one that exists. In the process, of course, you may be distorting the balance of interests and limiting the range of original potential response. If either of these things has happened, the evidence of public taste at any one time in relation to actually provided services cannot be taken as proving anything about people's needs and capacities.

In many known areas, a liking for certain kinds of thing already exists: this is where the trend starts from. But in a society like ours, changing in many ways, there are many unknown areas. Dr Silvey, Head of BBC Audience Research, has said:

The mass media do very largely confirm ideas which are already structured and held, but when it comes to spheres where there is a great deal of confusion, you cannot reinforce something which is not there, and it is in those kinds of areas where I think responsibility is at its greatest.

This is very important, because in the new kinds of living now opening up to us, many of our ideas and our tastes are bound to be potential. If meeting these is not kept in balance with meeting the ideas and tastes we already have, which can be quickly and easily served, the whole process of growth and change is likely to be damaged.

Very few people would disagree with the argument that this situation requires great responsibility. Mr King and Mr Collins both mentioned their attempts to raise standards, and to create new interests. The important question is whether the organization and the ruling ideas of mass communications as we know them are adequate for this very difficult job.

I believe them to be inadequate, for these reasons. First, while we go on talking about 'the masses' we can have neither the respect for people nor the sense of growth that underlie responsibility. Second, while we go on thinking in a separatist way about 'classes' – whether social groupings or such educational groupings as 'the academic type', 'the technical type', 'the operative whose interests are all in his hands' – we cannot have sufficiently flexible ideas about people, and will be constantly tempted to divide our culture into separate areas with no bridges between them. Third, while there is an emphasis on profit, there will be a constant pressure to concentrate on things already known and safe, with never enough effort given to the much longer and more difficult job of trying new things and offering new ideas and experience. Fourth, while there is an emphasis on using the channels as a medium for advertising and selling, there will be a constant pressure to get people into 'the right frame of mind for buying', and to use the appeal of known tastes as a jumping-off ground for directing new interests and new opportunities into channels convenient to those with something ready to sell, but not necessarily relevant to the real problems of the new living itself.

The question of 'giving the public what it wants' has to be looked at, then, not by one rough-and-ready rule, but in this more general and varied way.

HIGH AND LOW

Men differ in their capacities for excellence. Yet democracy insists that everyone has an equal right to judge. Aren't we seeing, in our own time, the results of this contradiction? Isn't there great danger of the tradition of high culture being overwhelmed by mass culture, which expresses the tastes and standards of the ordinary man? Isn't it really our first duty to defend minority culture, which in its actual works is the highest achievement of humanity?

The difficulty here is that 'minority culture' can mean two things. It can mean the work of the great artists and thinkers, and of the many lesser but still important figures who sustain them. It can mean also the work of these men as received and used by a particular social minority, which will indeed often add to it certain works and habits of its own.

The great tradition is in many ways a common

inheritance, and it has been the purpose of modern education to make it as widely available as possible. Certainly this extension is never as easy as some people expect. Certainly it often happens that in the attempt to make difficult work more widely available, part of the value of the work is lost. Perhaps the whole attempt is wrongly conceived, and we should concentrate instead on maintaining the high tradition in its own terms.

The question is, however, can this in any case be done? The work of the great artists and thinkers has never been confined to their own company; it has always been made available to some others. And doesn't it often happen that those to whom it has been made available identify the tradition with themselves, grafting it into their own way of life? Thus, Sophocles, Shakespeare, Ibsen, Shaw, Rattigan may be a true succession, or it may not. The latest terms are always subject to error. Not every man under the towers of Oxford or Cambridge is the fellow of Cranmer, Newman, and Arnold, and these names cannot really be used to show that he is doing more important work, belongs more to the high tradition, than a teacher in a school at Croydon or a writer on the remote island of Jura. Yet, again and again, particular minorities confuse the superiority of the tradition which has been made available to them with their own superiority, an association which the passing of time or of frontiers can make suddenly ludicrous. We must always be careful to distinguish the great works of the past from the social minority which at a particular place and time identifies itself with them.

The great tradition very often continues itself in quite unexpected ways. Much new work, in the past, has been called 'low', in terms of the 'high' standards of the day. This happened to much of our Elizabethan drama, and to the novel in the eighteenth century. Looking back, we can understand this, because the society was changing in fundamental ways. The minorities which assumed that they alone had the inheritance and guardianship of the great tradition in fact turned out to be wrong. This mistake can happen at any time. In our own century, there are such new forms as the film, the musical, and jazz. Each of these has been seen as 'low', a threat to 'our' standards. Yet during the period in which films have been made, there have been as many major contributions, in film, to the world's dramatic tradition, as there have been major plays. Of course most films are nowhere near this level. But from the past we have only the best work, and we can properly compare with this only our own best work. Some forms may well be better than others, in that they contain much greater possibilities for the artist, but this cannot be settled until there has been time for development. The great period of the novel came more than a century after the form had become popular and had been dismissed as 'low'. It realized possibilities which nobody could then have foreseen. The prestige of an old form is never decisive. There is no reason, today, why a science-fiction story should be thought less serious than an historical novel, or a new musical than a naturalist play. 'Low' equals 'unfamiliar' is one of the perennial cultural traps, and it is fallen into most easily by those who assume that in their own persons, in their own learned tastes and habits, they are the high tradition.

This might be agreed, but does it go to the real issue? These mistakes are made, but new minorities set them right. Still, however, they are minorities. Most people are not interested in the great tradition, old or new. Most people are not interested in art, but merely in entertainment. Actual popular taste is for such things as variety, the circus, sport, and processions. Why force art on such people, especially since you will be in danger of reducing art to that level, mixing it up with the popular and commercial worlds? Wouldn't your effort be better spent on maintaining real art for those who value it?

This distinction between art and entertainment may be much more difficult to maintain than it looks. At its extremes, of course, it is obvious. But over the whole range, is there any easy and absolute distinction? Great art can give us deep and lasting experiences, but the experience we get from many things that we rightly call art is quite often light and temporary. The excitement of the circus, the procession, the variety sketch, can be quite easily forgotten, but at the time it is often intense. Sport, in our century, has become a popular spectacle: its excitements again are intense and often temporary. There may be a difference between such things and the minor decorative arts, the passing comedies, the fashionable artistic performers, but can it really be seen as a difference between 'high' and 'low'? And even where the difference seems absolute, what follows from this? What has to be shown, to sustain the argument that 'high culture' is in danger of being overwhelmed by 'mass culture', is that there is not only difference but conflict. Most of us can test this in our own experience. For, in fact, we do not live in these neatly separated worlds. Many of us go one day to a circus, one day to a theatre; one day to the football, one day to a concert. The experiences are different, and vary widely in quality both between and within themselves. Do we in fact feel that our capacity for any one of these things is affected by our use of the others?

But perhaps this is not the main point. Isn't the real

threat of 'mass culture' – of things like television rather than things like football or the circus – that it reduces us to an endlessly mixed, undiscriminating, fundamentally bored reaction? The spirit of everything, art and entertainment, can become so standardized that we have no absorbed interest in anything, but simply an indifferent acceptance, bringing together what Coleridge called 'indulgence of sloth and hatred of vacancy'. You're not exactly enjoying it, or paying any particular attention, but it's passing the time. And in so deadly an atmosphere the great tradition simply cannot live.

Most of us, I think, have experienced this atmosphere. At times, even, we take it as a kind of drug: in periods of tiredness or convalescence, or during tension and anxiety when we have to wait and when almost anything can help us to wait. Certainly as a normal habit of mind this would be enervating and dangerous; there is a lot of reality that we cannot afford to be cut off from, however much we may want some temporary relief.

The challenge of work that is really in the great tradition is that in many different ways it can get through with an intensity, a closeness, a concentration that in fact move us to respond. It can be the reporter breaking through our prejudice to the facts; the dramatist reaching so deeply into our experience that we find it difficult, in the first shock, even to breathe; the painter suddenly showing us the shape of a street so clearly that we ask how we could ever have walked down it indifferently. It is sometimes a disturbing challenge to what we have always believed and done, and sometimes a way to new experience, new ways of seeing and feeling. Or again, in unexpected ways, it can confirm and strengthen us, giving new energy to what we already know is important, or what we knew but couldn't express.

Is this living world threatened by the routines of 'mass culture'? The threat is real, but it does not come only from 'mass culture'; it comes also from many kinds of routine art and routine thinking. There are many sources for the formula or routine which insulates us from reality. There is the weakness in ourselves, or at best the insufficient strength. There is also the intention of others, that we should be kept out of touch. Many interests are served by this kind of insulation: old forms of society, old and discredited beliefs, a wish to keep people quiet and uncritical. Such interests, based on power, habit, or privilege, are often served by, often actively seek, formulas and routines that insulate men from reality.

If we look at what we call 'mass culture' and 'minority culture', I am not sure that we invariably find one on the side of reality and one against it. Certainly the great works always challenge us with their own reality, and can stimulate us to active attention. But when these works are embedded in a particular minority culture, which adds to them not only its own local habits but also the facts and feelings which spring from its minority position, the effect can be very different. At best, a minority culture, in keeping the works available, offers the best that has been done and said in the world. At worst, it translates the best into its own accents, and confuses it with many other inferior things. I see no real evidence that it is a permanent and reliable means of maintaining a living excellence.

But even if it isn't permanent and reliable, isn't it bound to be better than the ordinary world of mass communications? There the construction of formulas seems almost built in. It is perhaps the only easy way of getting through quickly to a very large number of people, and the system seems to depend on this.

Certainly we can only understand large-scale communications if we acknowledge the importance of formulas which can be fairly quickly and widely learned and used. Yet, in fact, formulas are necessary for all communication. What is at worst a formula for processing an experience is at best a convention for transmitting it in a widely available form. We have seen so much falsification, glamorization, and real vulgarization that we often forget how many facts, how many new opinions, how many new kinds of work and new ways of seeing the world nevertheless get through. By comparison with times when there was no highly organized communications system these are dramatic gains. We have then to adjust the balance much more carefully than a simple contrast of 'minority' and 'mass', 'high' and 'low' would suggest.

There is one further argument, that can very easily be overlooked. The great tradition is itself always in danger of being vulgarized when it is confined to a minority culture. Just because it is a mixed inheritance, from many societies and many times as well as from many kinds of men, it cannot easily be contained within one limited social form. Further, if it is so contained, there can be deep and unnecessary hostility to it from those outside the social minority. If the great tradition is not made generally available, there is often this frightening combination of hostility and a vacuum. What then usually happens is that this is penetrated and exploited from outside. In the worst cultural products of our time, we find little that is genuinely popular, developed from the life of actual communities. We find instead a synthetic culture, or anti-culture, which is alien to almost everybody, persistently hostile to art and intellectual activity, which it spends much of its time in misrepresenting, and given over to exploiting indifference, lack of feeling, frustration, and hatred. It finds such common human interests as sex, and turns them into crude caricatures or glossy facsimiles. It plays repeatedly around hatred and aggression, which it never discharges but continually feeds. This is not the culture of 'the ordinary man'; it is the culture of the disinherited. It seems to me that those who have contrived the disinheritance, by artificially isolating the great tradition, bear as heavy a responsibility for these destructive elements as their actual providers.

In Britain, we have to notice that much of this bad work is American in origin. At certain levels, we are culturally an American colony. But of course it is not the best American culture that we are getting, and the import and imitation of the worst has been done, again and again, by some of our own people, significantly often driven by hatred or envy of the English minority which has associated the great tradition with itself. To go pseudo-American is a way out of the English complex of class and culture, but of course it solves nothing; it merely ritualizes the emptiness and despair. Most bad culture is the result of this kind of social collapse. The genuinely popular tradition is despised, the great tradition is kept exclusive, and into the gap pour the speculators who know how to exploit disinheritance because they themselves are rooted in nothing.

The general situation is very difficult to understand. In part, now, the great tradition is being responsibly extended, and is finding an excellent response, both in the real increase of audiences, and in the answering vitality of new contributions to it from new kinds of experience. The purely destructive exploitation of the vacuum is also very powerful, in part because the control of our cultural organization has passed very largely into the hands of men who know no other definitions. At the same time, against all the apparent odds, elements of the really popular tradition persist, especially in variety, sport, some kinds of spectacle, and the impulse to make our own entertainment, especially in music. It seems impossible to understand this many-sided and constantly changing situation through the old formulas of 'minority' and 'mass', which are the symptoms of the collapse rather than keys to understanding it. We have to look at a new situation in new ways.

VIOLENCE AND VALUES

Is there too much emphasis, in the popular Sunday newspapers, in television drama, and in the production and advertising of films, on 'violence' and 'sex'? That the emphasis is there can hardly be denied. But what kind of emphasis is it, and what are its actual or probable effects?

Who knows?

A fair amount of research has been carried out, in some fields, particularly in relation to 'violence'. Three kinds of question have been asked. How many items involving violence appear, as a proportion of total output? What attitudes to violence appear in these items? Are there cases where the apparent moral attitude is contradicted by the actual presentation?

The first question is easily answered, though it has never been looked at in a continuous way and over the whole communications field. There have been such counts as that of 7,065 acts or threats of violence on the television programmes of New York City in one week. In Britain a count of programmes on television, by the Council for Children's Welfare in a sample week, showed the following:

Family viewing hours (6–9 p.m.)	: 21 hours
ITV 'crime' and 'Westerns'	: $5\frac{1}{2}$ hours
BBC 'crime' and 'Westerns'	: $2\frac{1}{4}$ hours

Current figures, for programmes involving crime and violence, in the whole schedules offered, are:

BBC 1	: 6 hours 5 minutes
ITV	: 6 hours 35 minutes
BBC 2	: 4 hours 20 minutes

These amount to some eleven per cent (BBC 1), eleven per cent (ITV) and thirteen per cent (BBC 2), of all material shown. Of the hours stated, the following are in family viewing periods (6–9 p.m. weekdays, weekend afternoons and early evenings): BBC 1, $4\frac{1}{4}$ hours; ITV, $2\frac{3}{4}$ hours; BBC 2, $2\frac{1}{2}$ hours.

It is important to know such figures, but they are sometimes difficult to interpret. It is often argued that it is not the appearance of violence that matters, but the attitude to it within the work. On the other hand, the place of any one theme, however handled, within the general distribution of interests in the culture as a whole, is surely also important. Simple 'quantity counts' can be useful in showing this distribution of interests. If it is argued, for example, that 'violence ought to appear because it is a part of real life', it is relevant to ask its proportion in real life as compared with its proportion in newspapers, films, and television programmes. Any count in our own society would show that the proportion in communications is much higher than the proportion in the rest of our living. We should then ask not only why this is so, but what other interests are reduced or excluded to allow this altered proportion.

The second question, on attitudes to violence, has produced some detailed work. The most useful is that recorded in *Television and the Child*. There, for example, the difference between 'Westerns' and 'crime plays' is defined as a difference between stylization and black-and-white simplicity in the former, complexity and 'realism' in the latter. In moral attitudes, 'the central lesson of Westerns is that good triumphs over bad through violence – the manly, as well as the only, course of action. The villain's case is never stated, no sympathy is invited for him, and the hero never gains anything from his deeds. There is no suggestion of internal conflict or indecision.' In crime stories, there are three kinds of explicit values: 'First, that crime does not pay, because the law has vast resources. . . . Second, that the activities of criminals and the law are not in fact dissimilar. Both sides bully and cheat if necessary. . . . Third, that appearances are deceptive; a person may look harmless and yet be a criminal (though hardly ever the other way round). . . . Man is often not responsible for his deeds . . . he cannot help himself. While the law must be upheld, the criminal can yet evoke sympathy.' A further general difference between 'Westerns' and 'crime plays' is that in the former 'the impact of violence is dulled because there are no close-ups at the kill and also because the emphasis is on opposing sides rather than individuals'. In crime plays 'there is no attempt to evade the consequences of violence, the camera stays with a man who has been hit; we see blood on his hands and beads of sweat on his face . . . detailed expressions of physical pain'.

The third question, on possible differences between explicit attitudes and those actually embodied, has been too little studied. Yet it is important because the argument about effects can become naïve if only the formal 'moral' or 'lesson' is looked at. Thus, the regular message of crime plays that 'crime does not pay' may in fact be begging the question of what 'paying' really is. That the criminal is caught may be one conclusion. That in the process of his crime there has been 'pay' and satisfaction may often be another. The whole moral effect can then be deeply confused. On disturbing human themes, it is possible and even probable that there will often be conflict between the formal moral ending or moral intention and the actual experience most strongly expressed. Thus analysis of an American film against racial prejudice found that 'fantasies from a less conscious level come to the surface', expressing deep prejudices in a powerful way and making the effect of the whole film ambiguous.*

There is controversy over the results of these various kinds of content analysis. There is even more controversy over the effects of the content itself. Thus Mr Noel Stevenson, of Independent Television, said:

We have been talking about things like violence and immorality. As soon as you suggest that television can make people violent or make them immoral you are at once dealing with an area of values on which there are enormous social pressures – our home, our neighbourhood, our religious groups, our industrial groups – all, virtually speaking, are against violence, against immorality. I think myself that television has very little effect in any of these fields.

Dr Mark Abrams, sociologist, has said:

The abundance of this noxious material in the mass media is beyond dispute. But does it lead to direct, imitative behaviour on the part of ordinary average children? . . . Does it create among them a general climate of undesirable values? The available evidence from research on these points among children is slight and often negative. It appears that when maladjusted and welladjusted children are exposed to identical amounts of violent mass-media content, the former, unlike the latter, show a marked preference for such material, derive distinctive satisfactions from it, and, in the process of

* *Audio-Visual Communication Review*, Gerbner, Vol. 6, No. 2, Spring, 1958.

consumption, their problems are sustained rather than resolved. Since media violence, in some way as yet unknown to us, apparently intensifies the difficulties of maladjusted and frustrated children, a strong case can be made out for removing such material. The strength of the case, however, depends very largely on two considerations: first, how large is the proportion of our children who are maladjusted and frustrated? If it is very low, e.g. 1 or 2 per cent, then the introduction of censorship could hardly be justified; while if it is high, e.g. 20 or 25 per cent, then the case would seem to be unanswerable. Unfortunately, this is yet another area where, in spite of the abundance of debate, we lack any reliable, relevant facts. We do not know whether it is 2 per cent or 22 per cent.

Dr Hilde Himmelweit, psychologist, has said:

If, year after year, one gives children a diet in which these elements feature rather largely . . . there is no question that their view of society, that violence is a rather ordinary thing, that conflicts can best be solved by physical violence, may gradually make an impact on the children. I would have thought this was not a risk worth taking.

Who cares?

The question is not only 'who knows?' It is also 'who cares?' To prove the effects of any particular kind of work is difficult, if not impossible, because anyone exposed to that work will also have been exposed to a whole range of other experience, from which the effects of the work itself cannot easily be separated. At the same time, this difficulty applies to almost everything that society seeks to control or forbid or encourage. In the end, decisions of this kind are made either from the standards of a ruling group, or from the general conscience of the society, which may often have been aroused by a crusading minority. It is important that allegations of danger, or possible danger, should be critically examined in the light of the best knowledge we have. But it is wrong to suppose that the only argument now current is that between people who make different estimates of this kind of risk. Behind this argument is another body of opinion, which is not thinking in these terms at all. The proprietors and editors of popular Sunday newspapers and comics, the publishers and authors of 'sex-and-violence' novels, the controllers and producers of similar television programmes, the producers and advertisers of similar films, do not base their activity on an estimate of the danger of their work to the public and, having found it non-existent or negligible, go ahead. Their principle is the quite different one that if such work will sell or is popular it is all right to provide it. It is here that the second question arises: who cares?

The whole argument would be easier if those who do care were all of the same kind. Through all the differences of interpretation, there is a similar kind of concern among teachers, among many parents, among social welfare bodies, and among sociologists, psychologists, and writers. But overlapping their arguments, and sometimes resembling them, are the complaints of those who are judging one generation by the standards of another, who ask 'My Lords, where are we going?' or 'What on earth are we coming to, in this degraded modern world?' The confusion was interestingly illustrated by the argument about the publication of *Lady Chatterley's Lover*.

For some people, at one extreme, the argument was simple: 'Let us get rid of these old-fashioned restrictions, this self-punishing Puritanism. People should be able to read what they want to, and artists of course must be free to write what they want to.' For others, at the opposite extreme, the argument was also simple: 'The Christian virtues of our children are being violated in order to fill the ever-bulging pockets of unscrupulous publishers with gold filched from the virtues of our children.' *Lady Chatterley's Lover* was seen as of a piece with cheap pornography, suggestive films, horror-comics, and violence on television.

The more difficult position was that of people who used one argument – 'the artist's freedom to publish' – in defence of Lawrence, and another argument – 'the duty of society to protect the immature' – in criticism of the Sunday newspapers and television violence. I do not really see how both these arguments can be honestly used. I am sure that *Lady Chatterley's Lover* is in a wholly different class, as art, from the great bulk of popular work. I am sure also, in my own mind, that it would do good where other work does harm. But, as a matter of general principle, we cannot rely on absolute contrasts between good and bad work; there will always be work that is mixed or intermediate. If we stand on 'freedom to publish', we shall not in fact be able to confine this to moral masterpieces. If we stand on 'protecting the immature', we shall have to accept that in fact all work, good, bad, and indifferent, will have to undergo this scrutiny. It is argued that effect can be judged in terms of the kind of audience addressed: something all right for adults would be wrong for children. This may be generally true, but in practice it seems that it is impossible to confine most work to any one group: whatever the intention, the actual audiences to some extent overlap, quite apart from the natural overlap of adolescence. Moreover, within each audience, whether of adults, adolescents, or children, there will be wide differences of character and stability which may have everything to do with the actual effect. A psychopathic adult may be more easily affected, and may as a result do more damage, than a very young but secure child.

We need more evidence on this whole question, but is

it right, if a matter is urgent, to go on waiting for more evidence, and, if so, for how long? Action is in any case already being taken: many things are being distributed, many things are being banned or clipped. The real questions seem to be: Who makes the decisions, to distribute or to ban? On what grounds are these made or publicly justified? It may be very difficult to find the best possible system, either in institutions or in values, but, as Carlyle said, 'If you ask which is the worst, I answer, this which we now have, that chaos should sit umpire in it; this is the worst.' For we have evidently not made up our minds between the competing cries, 'freedom to publish', 'duty to be responsible', 'what's wanted should be provided', 'perversion or confusion of our values'. Until we are clear about this, and have some real principles and procedures, which we are prepared to recognize over the whole field, the chaos, and any possible damage, will continue.

THE CONTRIBUTORS

Surely the people who really matter, in any culture, are the active contributors. Why do we talk always about publics and audiences and cultural systems? Surely the only way to get good culture is to have good artists and performers. And is there really anything we can do about getting them? Perhaps the most we can do is to try to create a society in which artists find it worth living.

Certainly the contributors are of the first importance. But can we really assume that they are all of the same kind, with the same general needs? And can we also assume that different publics and systems have no effect on the sort of contributors we actually get?

We can distinguish four main kinds of contributor: the creative artist, the performer, the reporter, the commentator or critic. Each of these has, in the first instance, a direct responsibility to his work. It is true that each is trying to communicate this work to others. It is obviously desirable that each should try to make this communication as successful as possible. But, in the act of work itself, there is a special kind of responsibility. To understand this we have to look more closely at what communication involves.

A reporter gets at certain facts. A commentator or critic gives his opinion of an actual event or work. A performer expresses, in his own medium, a work created by himself or another. A creative artist seeks to embody in a work his own experience or vision. Each sees his work differently, but certain factors are common. Each, even the artist, is trying to put his work into a communicable form. Yet each can only communicate, with any real satisfaction, on the basis of what he actually finds necessary to say or show. It is no use thinking 'If I altered it, they would understand it more easily', because while it might then be easier to get in touch with others, it might no longer be getting in touch on the basis of what actually needs to be said.

This reality defines the freedom of cultural contribution. In their different ways, the reporter, the commentator and critic, the performer, and the artist need a guaranteed freedom to communicate what, in terms of *their own* understanding of their work, needs to be communicated. This sounds like, and is, a definition of individual freedom. But it is not only for the sake of individuals that this freedom should be guaranteed. A good society depends on the free availability of facts and opinions, and on the growth of vision and consciousness – the articulation of what men have actually seen and known and felt. Any restriction of the freedom of individual contribution is actually a restriction of the resources of the society.

How is the communication actually achieved? It depends, of course, either on a common language or on known conventions, or at least on the beginnings of these. If the common language and the conventions exist, the contributor tries to use them as well as he can. But often, especially with original artists and thinkers, the problem is in one way that of creating a language, or creating a convention, or at least of developing the language and conventions to the point where they are capable of bearing his precise meaning. In literature, in music, in the visual arts, in the sciences, in social thinking, in philosophy, this kind of development has occurred again and again. It often takes a long time to get through, and for many people it will remain difficult. But we need never think that it is impossible; creative energy is much more powerful than we sometimes suppose. While any man is engaged in this struggle to say new things in new ways, he is usually more than ever concentrated on the actual work, and not on its possible audience. Many artists and scientists share this fundamental unconcern about the ways in which their work will be received. They may be glad if it is understood and appreciated, hurt if it is not, but while the work is being done there can be no argument. The thing has to come out as the man himself sees it.

In this sense it is true that it is the duty of society to create conditions in which such men can live. For whatever the value of any individual contribution, the general body of work is of immense value to everyone. But of course things are not so formal, in reality. There is not society on the one hand and these individuals on the other. In ordinary living, and in his work, the contributor shares in the life of his society, which often affects him both in minor ways and in ways sometimes so deep that he is not even aware of them. His ability to make his work public depends on the actual communication system: the language itself, or certain visual or musical or scientific conventions, and the institutions through which the communication will be passed. The effect of these on his actual work can be almost infinitely variable. For it is not only a communication system outside him; it is also, however original he may be, a communication system which is in fact part of himself. Many contributors make active use of this kind of internal communication system. It is to themselves, in a way, that they first show their conceptions, play their music, present their arguments. Not only as a way of getting these clear, in the process of almost endless testing that active composition involves. But also, whether consciously or not, as a way of putting the experience into a communicable form. If one mind has grasped it, even if only the mind that also created it, then it may be open to other minds.

In this deep sense, the society is in some ways already present in the act of composition. This is always very difficult to understand, but often, when we have the advantage of looking back at a period, we can see, even if we cannot explain, how this was so. We can see how much even highly original individuals had in common, in their actual work, with other individual workers of the time, and with the society of that time to which they belonged. The historian is also continually struck by the fact that men of this kind felt isolated at the very time when in reality they were beginning to get through. This can also be noticed in our own time, when some of the most deeply influential men feel isolated and even rejected. The society and the communication are there, but it is difficult to recognize them, difficult to be sure.

When we turn to institutions, we need to remember this deep social reality of communication. For if we do not, we can be easily tempted into one of two very common false positions. Either we can say that we should leave the contributors alone, because they are so important: a form of flattery which in fact comes through as neglect, leaving men already at the limits of their strength to the doubtful mercy of every wind that blows. The contributors are involved in their society, both in profound ways and in their ordinary human needs, and they usually suffer if they are cut off from it, whether as 'impractical dreamers' or as 'untouchable spirits'. Or we can say, as so many now do, that the institutions of communication should be defined first, and then the contributors fitted into them. We have seen this happen so often that it is sometimes the only danger we are aware of. It is certainly a constant and serious danger. Power can say to the reporter: 'Remember what kind of paper this is; if you want to work on it, learn its ways'. Or to the commentator and critic: 'Remember on what beliefs this society is based; express your opinion by all means, but of course within these beliefs.' Or to the performer: 'What in fact we like to see is this; you're a talented person, you could surely learn.' Or to the artist: 'Of course creative people are a bit temperamental, they get wrapped up in themselves, but think of the good you could do, think of the people you could reach, if you did this and not that.' Many contributors, of course, will do as they are told. Some, though, will cry from the depths: 'Leave me alone, let me get on with my work.' And then, in the next breath, paradoxically: 'Why are the really creative people always ignored and neglected?'

Is there any way between these opposite errors? Well, there is a clear difference between those contributors who cannot work at all without institutions (film and television companies, theatres, orchestras, newspapers, and magazines), and those who are not so immediately dependent (writers, composers, painters, sculptors) though in the end institutions affect them. In each of these kinds, there are many who compromise early: learning to produce exactly what the institution wants, or learning how to satisfy the market. The pressures are often so great, in the absence of any alternative policy, that this seems bound to happen in very many cases. Of those who stand out for their own work, those least immediately dependent are obviously in the stronger position, and their view of the matter is often received with impatience by those who cannot even work unless an institution is found. Nevertheless, they have kept alive a principle which is of general importance. However arrogant it sounds in particular cases, especially when made by one man on behalf of his own work, it remains true that a contributor's freedom to work on his own terms is a gain to society as a whole. The only useful institutions, in cultural organization, are those which are designed to guarantee this freedom. Such arrangements will vary according to the work, and in the case of those contributors not immediately dependent on institutions, the more informal they are the better. But in other cases, and even for the most individual contributors, institutions of a kind will in any case be there. Behind the proclamation of the freedom of the reporter and the artist, real freedom, in many cases, has dramatically declined, as official and commercial organization has become tighter and more pervasive. It is no longer useful merely to proclaim this freedom. What matters is to work out its practical means. In this, the contributors need the support of the wider public. I do not think this support will be gained, in practice (it is gained without difficulty in theory, which costs nothing), unless the arguments for freedom of contribution are put on a wider basis. Simply saying 'leave me alone' may produce exactly that result: the nonconformists will be left alone, while the conformists take over the whole culture. Yet, if we understand the real process of communication, the contributor's freedom and his need for control over his own resources can be reasonably seen as a means to freedom in the whole society, and as the best way in which the contributor can serve the society. From the freedom of the contributor, properly understood, can spring the real relations with society on which he also depends.

We might usefully remember some words of Blake. He suffered through most of his life from neglect and the vagaries of the market, and he was a profoundly original poet and artist. He seems to me to have cut through a world of fashionable cant with this direct and wise conclusion:

> Some People & not a few Artists have asserted that the Painter of this Picture would not have done so well if he had been properly Encourag'd. Let those who think so, reflect on the State of Nations under Poverty & their incapability of Art; tho' Art is above either, the Argument is better for Affluence than Poverty; & tho' he would not have been a greater Artist, yet he would have produced Greater works of Art in proportion to his means.

THE SYSTEMS

Perhaps it comes down to this: either the communication system is controlled or it is free. In a democracy there can be no argument on this point: the system must be free or there is no democracy. In a free system many of the things produced may be bad or offensive, or may seem bad and offensive to some people. But the only alternative is a controlled system, or monopoly, in which some people are imposing their tastes on others. 'In fact,' said Sir Robert Fraser, Head of the

Independent Television Authority, defending the introduction of commercial television, 'the old system of monopoly in Britain was carried away by a wave of democratic thought and feeling.'

It would be easy to score debating points against Sir Robert Fraser: to ask, for example, what 'a wave of democratic thought and feeling' has in common with the actual process of pressure-group lobbying, much of it by persons with a direct financial interest, which got commercial television through. But this is not the main issue, since behind all the detail of contemporary controversy lies an evident conflict of principles, which has to be faced and understood.

In one way, the basic choice is between control and freedom, but in actual terms it is more often a choice between a measure of control and a measure of freedom, and the substantial argument is about how these can be combined. Further, the bare words 'controlled' and 'free' do not seem sufficiently precise, in themselves, to describe the kinds of communication system which we have had or known about or wanted. I believe that we can distinguish four main kinds, and that to describe and compare these will make our thinking about control and freedom more realistic. The four kinds are: authoritarian, paternal, commercial, and democratic.

Authoritarian

In this system, communications are seen as part of the total machine through which a minority governs a society. The first purpose of communication is to transmit the instructions, ideas, and attitudes of the ruling group. As a matter of policy, alternative instructions, ideas, and attitudes are excluded. Monopoly of the means of communication is a necessary part of the whole political system: only certain printers, publishing houses, newspapers, theatres, broadcasting stations will be allowed. Sometimes these will be directly controlled by the ruling group, who will then directly decide what is transmitted. At other times, a more indirect control will be completed by a system of censorship, and often by a system of political and administrative action against sources unfavourable to those in power.

Such a system can operate with varying degrees of severity, and in the interest of several different kinds of society. We can see it in past periods in Britain as clearly as in modern totalitarian states. The distinguishing characteristic of such a system is that the purpose of communication is to protect, maintain, or advance a social order based on minority power.

Paternal

A paternal system is an authoritarian system with a conscience: that is to say, with values and purposes beyond the maintenance of its own power. Authoritarians, on various grounds, claim the right to rule. In a paternal system, what is asserted is the duty to protect and guide. This involves the exercise of control, but it is a control directed towards the development of the majority in ways thought desirable by the minority. If monopoly of the means of communication is used, it is argued that this is to prevent the means being abused by groups which are destructive or evil. Censorship is widely used, in such a system, both directly and indirectly, but it is defended on the grounds that certain groups and individuals need, in their own interest and in the public interest, protection against certain kinds of art or ideas which would be harmful to them. Where the authoritarian system transmits orders, and the ideas and attitudes which will promote their acceptance, the paternal system transmits values, habits, and tastes, which are its own justification as a ruling minority, and which it wishes to extend to the people as a whole. Criticism of such values, habits, and tastes will be seen as at best a kind of rawness and inexperience, at worst a moral insurrection against a tried and trusted way of life. The controllers of a paternal system see themselves as guardians. Though patient, they must be uncompromising in defence of their central values. At the same time, the proper discharge of their duty requires a high sense of responsibility and seriousness. At different times, and serving different social orders, the paternal system can vary in the degree to which it explicitly announces its role or explains its methods. The actual methods can also vary widely: sometimes putting the blanket over everything; sometimes allowing a measure of controlled dissent or tolerance as a safety-valve. But the general purpose and atmosphere of the system remain unmistakable.

Commercial

The commercial attitude to communications is powerfully opposed to both authoritarianism and paternalism. Instead of communication being for government or for guidance, it is argued that men have the right to offer for sale any kind of work, and that all men have the right to buy any kind that is offered. In this way, it is claimed, the freedom of communication is assured. You do not have to ask anybody's leave to publish or to read. Works are openly offered for sale and openly bought, as people actually choose.

In its early stages, and in some of its later stages, such a system is certainly a means to freedom by comparison with either of the former systems. But since this freedom depends on the market it can run into difficulties. Can a work be offered for sale if there is no certainty that people will in fact buy it? When production is cheap, this risk will often be taken. When production is expensive, it may not be. In a modern system of communications many kinds of production are inevitably expensive. What, then, happens to the simple original principle? First: works whose sale is uncertain, or likely to be very small in relation to cost, may not be offered at all. Second: speed of sale becomes an important factor – it is not easy to wait for years for a return on a very large investment if the act of buying and selling is the most important consideration. Investment elsewhere might bring much quicker returns. Third: if the amount of capital needed to finance a work is large, there can be no free offering for sale, as in the original principle. Individual artists will almost certainly not possess the necessary capital. They have then to be financed by individuals or groups with such capital, and it is probable that considerations of extent or speed of sale, and so of return or profit on the investment, will be decisive as to whether such an offer of financing is made. But then practical control of the means of communication, over large areas and particularly in the more expensive kinds, can pass to individuals or groups whose main, if not only, qualification will be that they possess or can raise the necessary capital. Such groups, by the fact of this qualification, will often be quite unrepresentative of the society as a whole; they will be, in fact, a minority within it. Thus the control claimed as a matter of power by authoritarians, and as a matter of principle by paternalists, is often achieved as a matter of practice in the operation of the commercial system. Anything can be said, provided that you can afford to say it and that you can say it profitably.

Democratic

We have experienced the other three systems, but the democratic system, in any full sense, we can only discuss and imagine. It shares with the early commercial system a definition of communication which insists that all men have the right to offer what they choose and to receive what they choose. It is firmly against authoritarian control of what can be said, and against paternal control of what ought to be said. But also it is against commercial control of what can profitably be said, because this also can be a tyranny.

All proposals for new systems appear abstract, and at times unconvincing, because it is only when they are put into practice that they can be felt to be real. The working out of any democratic system will obviously be long and difficult, but what matters first is to define the general nature of a cultural system compatible with democracy, since there is only any chance of success in building it if enough of us can agree that this is the kind of thing we want.

There are two related considerations: the right to transmit and the right to receive. It must be the basis of any democratic culture, first, that these are basic rights; second, that they can never be tampered with by minorities; third, that if they are ever in any way limited, by some majority decision of the society, this can happen only after open and adequate public discussion, to which all are free to contribute and which will remain open to challenge and review.

On the right to transmit, the basic principle of democracy is that since all are full members of the society, all have the right to speak as they wish or find. This is not only an individual right, but a social need, since democracy depends on the active participation and the free contribution of all its members. The right to receive is complementary to this: it is the means of participation and of common discussion.

The institutions necessary to guarantee these freedoms must clearly be of a public-service kind, but it is very important that the idea of public service should not be used as a cover for a paternal or even authoritarian system. The idea of public service must be detached from the idea of public monopoly, yet remain public service in the true sense. The only way of achieving this is to create new kinds of institution.

The principle should be that the active contributors have control of their own means of expression. In the case of contributors not immediately dependent on institutions, this means guaranteeing them, if they want, certain facilities which will be their means of living and working. In cases where the work can only be done through institutions, it means creating the opportunity for the setting up, by various working groups, of their own companies, which will then be guaranteed the facilities they need. Some of these guarantees can be given by various intermediate institutions, themselves not dependent or directly dependent on the organs of government. But probably the greater part of the necessary resources will have to come directly from public funds. It is then necessary to create intermediate bodies, including representatives of the public and of the companies, to hold these public resources in trust for the society as a whole and for the needs of the various companies.

There should be no direct control by government over contributors. The creation of intermediate bodies, and of a contractual system by which individuals and companies are guaranteed certain resources for the work they want to do, can in practice make governmental control impossible, so long as the general life of the society remains democratic. In any system, if general democracy goes, cultural democracy will go too. But while there is general democracy (in defence of which an active cultural democracy is continually necessary) what matters most is a clear acceptance of the principle that the resources exist for the contributors to use for the work they themselves want to do, and that all decisions about the actual allocation of resources should be publicly argued and open to challenge and review.

There are two difficulties in this principle, certain also to be difficult in practice. The case for control by the contributors is that the society cannot by any means be better served than by giving the contributors their freedom and the necessary resources to work with. Control by functionless financial groups, or by political or administrative factions, is certain to be damaging. But will there, can there be no control at all: either by the allocation of resources to this work rather than that, or by any measures thought generally necessary to protect the public interest?

A democratic culture would need to allot considerable resources, to keep the first danger small. It would need in any case to resist any tendency to restrict work to its own channels, however adequate. If, even in the most enlightened system, an individual or a group cannot get support, it must be quite clear that there is nothing to stop them working in any way they can, and offering their work in any way they can: a situation in which they would be much as now. The more difficult aspect of this question is that a healthy culture depends on growth, yet at any given moment new kinds of work may command little interest, and there might be considerable public pressure to give them little or no support. How can this be overcome, in any democratic way? There is no simple answer, and the only possible answer is that if it is of the nature of democratic culture that it keeps the channels of growth clear, it is a public duty to see that individuals or groups offering new kinds of work are given at least a fair chance. The problem is really one of holding the ring, to give new work the time (it will often be a long time) to prove itself. The more varied the organization, the more independent companies there are, the more this chance is likely to be given.

The second difficulty is severe. We have seen how in certain cases it can be deeply held that there are certain things which ought not to be offered, because they are likely, on the available evidence, to harm people. Will not such restrictions have to be made? Even if they are publicly argued, publicly decided, and continually open to review, are they not still restrictions? Is not paternalism in some form necessary after all? In fact, of course, if it is a majority decision it is not paternalism. But it will still feel like it, to those affected. Again, there is no simple answer to this. The general issues, and all particular cases, need continual discussion. I believe that with the pressure of profit lifted there would be less work of this difficult kind. Yet there would always be some, and you might get a majority decision against serious work. The only way to prevent this is to promote the most open discussion, including the contributor's own reasoning, or reasoning on his behalf. I do not believe that, when this is done, people usually choose wrongly. In any event, one case lost is often the next case won, for in arguing the cases there is a real growth of understanding.

It seems to be best to let the contribution be made, and let the contributor take responsibility for it. The curious situation now, in a commercial culture, is that the contributor is often neither free nor responsible:

neither doing what he would independently have done, nor answerable to public criticism for what he has actually done. The balance inherent in democracy requires the creation of both these new conditions: freedom to do and freedom to answer, as an active process between many individuals.

SUMMARY

The four systems described, authoritarian, paternal, commercial, and democratic, are all to some extent active, in practice or in local experiment, in contemporary Britain. The vestiges of authoritarianism are there, in certain kinds of censorship; the first experiments in democracy are also there, in local ways. But the main struggle, over the last generation, has been between the paternal and commercial systems, and it looks as if the commercial has been steadily winning. It is most important, in this situation, that we should not confine the debate to the limited contrast of 'controlled' and 'free' systems, but instead should look over the whole range, and into detailed comparisons and possibilities.

5
Proposals

WHAT can be done? Should anything be done? We must answer these questions for ourselves, but in fact, if some of us decide to do nothing, this does not mean that the situation will stay as it is. No social process, in contemporary Britain, is more dynamic than this extension of communications. This means that there will in any case be further change, some of it of a very rapid and far-reaching kind. It may all seem too complicated or too powerful to touch. Or it may seem, on balance, to be going reasonably well, with such faults as there are so intractable that any attempt at cure might be worse than the disease. In any case, all possible courses of action have different motives: no action in this field is separate from action in the society as a whole, where there are deep and important disagreements. If we act, or try to act, we must state our reasons and our motives.

I stated my own position in *The Long Revolution*. I see this cultural revolution as part of a great process of human liberation, comparable in importance with the industrial revolution and the struggle for democracy. I want this process to continue, and I have no desire at all to go back, or try to go back, to any earlier stage of its history. I believe also that we must not see any part of this great process of change as separate, or as an end in itself. For, if we do, we run into contradictions of a severe kind — setting cultural difficulties against democracy, or setting cultural and democratic values against the industrial revolution. The essential values,

133

as I see them, are common to the whole process: that men should grow in capacity and power to direct their own lives – by creating democratic institutions, by bringing new sources of energy to human work, and by extending the expression and exchange of experience on which understanding depends.

Different societies will pursue these aims in different ways. In Britain, we start with a tradition which already, at its best, is firmly attached to this kind of progress. The aim has been there, in many minds, for several generations: to create an educated and participating democracy. We can achieve this only in terms of an advanced industrial society, and the community we are building is and must be a wholly new kind of community, in which the new kinds of communication – not only television and broadcasting and cheap books, but also greater mobility and greater opportunities to travel – must be not only taken into account, but welcomed. The growth of large-scale organization and communication is a major human gain, far outweighing the real difficulties and confusions it has also brought, and this extension needs to go much farther yet, towards a world community. Any action we take, then, should be in line with these aims. And we shall understand the whole process much better if we grasp it as part of a long and now almost universal historical movement, in which even in an advanced society like Britain we are still at a comparatively early stage.

In the stress of change there is a great deal of confusion. It is often argued that we can only meet this with an even greater emphasis on personal responsibility. This is true, provided we recognize that responsibility, in any real sense, is in any case continually changing. Indeed, part of the meaning of responsibility is the capacity to recognize and respond

to new situations. What is often meant, however, by
emphasis on personal responsibility, is that we sho
not do anything very much in the way of public change,
because that is comparatively superficial, whereas if
parents could only be responsible ('let them use the
freedom of the switch') there would be real strength.
This is a tragic under-estimate of the situation when it is
seriously offered, and a simple evasion of responsibility
when it is ordinarily offered. Personal choice is real and
necessary, but for just this reason we cannot really
choose for others. Even parents cannot, and in my view
ought not to, choose in this absolute way for their
children. The burden of wise choice needs an extension
of responsibility in which we can all share. If we want to
make the best of the new and real opportunities which
cultural extension provides, and if we want to avoid and
put right the mistakes which are in fact being made,
personal responsibility has to grow into public responsibility, which is a different and absolutely radical thing.

What forms can this public responsibility take? First,
in education, we can find new ways of developing the
capacity for personal and independent response and
choice. Second, in amendment of institutions, and in
legislation, we can make sure that our cultural
organization is, in real ways, responsible to the society
of which it is so important a part. Third, in new social
construction, we can propose and try to get agreement
for radical changes in institutions, to make them
adequate to the needs of a growing society.

I am setting down certain proposals in each of these
three fields. All need further discussion, and are offered
for discussion.

IN EDUCATION

We already teach communication, in certain ways, and

135

we also teach some practice and appreciation of the arts. Some of this work is good, but some of it is limited by assumptions taken over from old-fashioned ideas of culture and society, and some of it is even harmful.

Teaching speech

At the roots of much of our cultural thinking is our actual experience of speech. In Britain the question of good speech is deeply confused, and is in itself a major source of many of the divisions in our culture. It is inevitable, in modern society, that our regional speech-forms should move closer to each other, and that many extreme forms should disappear. But this should be a natural process, as people move and travel and meet more freely, and as they hear different speakers in films, television, and broadcasting. The mistake is to assume that there is already a 'correct' form of modern English speech, which can serve as a standard to condemn all others. In fact 'public-school English', in the form in which many have tried to fix it, cannot now become a common speech-form in the country as a whole: both because of the social distinctions now associated with its use, and because of the powerful influence of American speech-forms. Yet many good forms of modified regional speech are in practice emerging and extending. The barriers imposed by dialect are reduced, in these forms, without the artificiality of imitating a form remote from most people's natural speaking. This is the path of growth. Yet in much speech training, in schools, we go on assuming that there is already one 'correct' form over the country as a whole. Thousands of us are made to listen to our natural speaking with the implication from the beginning that it is *wrong*. This sets up such deep tensions, such active feelings of shame and resentment, that it should be no surprise that we cannot discuss culture in Britain without at once encountering tensions and prejudices deriving from this situation. If we experience speech training as an aspect of our social inferiority, a fundamental cultural division gets built in, very near the powerful emotions of self-respect, family affection, and local loyalty. This does not mean that we should stop speech training. But we shall not get near a common culture in Britain unless we make it a real social process – listening to ourselves and to others with no prior assumption of correctness – rather than the process of imitating a social class which is remote from most of us, leaving us stranded at the end with the 'two-language' problem. Nothing is more urgent than to get rid of this arbitrary association between general excellence and the habits of a limited social group. It is not only that there is much that is good elsewhere. It is also that, if you associate the idea of quality with the idea of class, you may find both rejected as people increasingly refuse to feel inferior on arbitrary social grounds.

Teaching writing

Here again we are faced with the problem of a necessary kind of training being limited by old ideas. It is not only that many of us are taught to write in old-fashioned styles. It is also that the forms we are taught often have little to do with the actual writing we need to practise.

In practice speaking, we are often limited to the formal debate or the casual three-minute speech, though neither, as taught, plays much real part in social life. We need to practise, therefore, such forms as the committee discussion, the verbal report, or the detailed questioning of a speech. Similarly, in writing, we need to practise not only the essay, but also the written report, the memorandum and minutes. One of the few common applied forms we now have is the business letter (perhaps not quite so terrible as it was, but still, as it comes through the post, pretty bad). We could do with regular practice in all kinds of correspondence – the letter of protest to the local paper as often as the acknowledgement of your 'kind favour'. We could also do with some practice in writing official forms, not only because so many are unnecessarily difficult, but also because their ordinary social tone is as regularly a kind of licensed bullying as that of the commercial letter is a kind of non-committal crawling. It would be something if we could learn to write to each other, on official or business occasions, in ways compatible with a self-respecting democratic society.

Teaching creative expression

Much of the best practice, in speech and writing, is and ought to be of a creative kind. In our junior schools, particularly, we have learned the value of making poems, stories, plays, figures, pictures, models, music, dance. Some of this work is excellent by any standards. Most of it is interesting. But the major limitation now built into this kind of teaching is that it is regarded as a form of *play*. This means that at a certain age it can be safely dropped, and put away with other childish things.

It is indeed play in the sense that most of us enjoy doing it. But these creative activities are also forms of work: for many adults, the work to which they give their whole lives. It is only the prejudice of a very narrow and early industrial society that the value of these activities is seen as a sort of harmless and indifferent play or therapy. From these activities comes much of man's real society, and they should be given that kind of respect throughout education. In the changes that come with puberty, it is vital that the practice of these activities should be continued, with no setting of 'more real' or 'more practical' work above them. Otherwise there is unnecessary fading, and all the major arts are relegated to the sphere of 'leisure': a separation which in itself makes inevitable, and much deeper than it ever now needs to be, a separation between art and society. Both sides then suffer: the arts because they are seen as marginal and specialized; society because it is limited to economics and administration. It is depressing to think that much of this division is now actively taught and learned in our schools, which at an earlier stage do so much to show how important and satisfying the arts can be to almost everyone.

Teaching contemporary arts

The proper extension of creative practice is direct experience and discussion of all the contemporary arts at their best. The difficulty here is the 'Goldsmith assumption': the idea that education has done its work when it has introduced us to a few classic authors. Of course we should get to know as much as we can of our inherited literature. But if we get to know it as a body of 'classics', we may sometimes confirm what is being taught elsewhere: that the arts are separate, in this case separate in time. It is significant how often, when culture is discussed, the idea of the museum is thrown in, often with real resentment.

In literature, to include contemporary work can have the good effect of unmaking the classics and remaking them as novels, poems, and plays. This is especially the case if living writers are invited into the educational process, at all possible stages, to read and talk about their work. Even if we can only get records of people reading their own work, the atmosphere is still quite different. Similarly, we need not confine experience of painting to standard reproductions on the walls of schools and colleges. Many artists would be glad to be invited, and the local exhibition of painting or sculpture, or the building actually designed, discussed, and built in our own town, is always the place to start learning. Already, in music, composers have proved very willing to travel and play and discuss their work. This kind of contact, with creative artists and performers, is important above all because of the spirit it communicates. We should be careful, moreover, not to play safe in these invitations: we should ask many kinds of creator and performer. The deepest danger, now, is the external division (pushed by the media, ratified by education) between those arts which are thought of as serious, academic, and old and those which are experienced as lively, personal, and new. To underwrite this division harms the traditional work and misses the chance of creating real standards in the new. In this respect, such new forms as jazz and the cinema are crucial. Yet for one school performance and discussion of a good contemporary film there seem to be hundreds of visits to films of 'the classics' – versions of Dickens and Shakespeare made respectable by that fact, yet often inferior, as cinema, to new work. And then good new work, as in jazz, is left mixed up in our minds with the bad work which our educational authorities think they are doing their duty by dismissing as inferior, negligible, and even dangerous. The resentment and confusion this causes has never been adequately appreciated. The only way to get some real movement and understanding is to bring in people who have actual standards, from their own work, and can communicate both its quality and its excitement.

Teaching the institutions

Because of the importance the institutions of communication now have in our society, we should include the teaching of certain basic facts about them in all our education. This should include something of their history and current social organization. It should include also some introduction to the ways in which they actually work.

The large impersonal media, such as the Press, the cinema, radio and television, come through to most people almost as acts of God. It is very difficult, without direct experience of their actual working, to see them as the products of men like ourselves. I know that since I have seen something of television and radio production, and of publishing, I have quite different attitudes to their finished work. It is a loss of naïvety but also in many ways a gain in respect: more critical, in every good sense, because more informed. If we are to feel that our communication system belongs to the society, instead of feeling that it is what 'they' have set up for us, this kind of understanding of method must grow.

To follow through the real processes in producing a newspaper, a magazine, a book, a radio discussion programme, a television play, a film, a dance, an opera, is usually exciting and invariably educative. Much more of this could be done by an intelligent use of modern resources. The only danger to avoid is the quite common substitute for this work, in the glamorized 'public relations' version of all these activities which is now so often put out. If it is to be valuable, this kind of teaching must base itself on the methods of education and not of publicity, especially since all our cultural institutions now suffer from the effects of this glamorized version, not only on others but on the people working in the tension between the glamour and the reality. (See Appendix A.)

Teaching criticism

That education should be critical of all cultural work is often the first point that springs to mind. Criticism is certainly essential, but for a number of reasons we have often done it so badly that there has been real damage. It is wholly wrong, for example, if education is associated with criticism while the non-educational world is associated with practice. Personal practice, direct experience of the arts, understanding of the institutions, should all come first. Or rather, criticism should develop as an aspect of each of these kinds of teaching, for it will always be bad if it is really separated from them. In teaching 'the classics' we are usually not critical enough. We often substitute a dull and inert 'appreciation' which nobody can go on believing in for long. But then in teaching or commenting on all other work, we are usually so confident and so fierce that it is difficult to believe we are the same people. 'All that muck in the cinemas and on television' too often follows the routine remarks on the charm of the *Essays of Elia*, and neither does anybody any good.

Our real purpose should be to bring all cultural work within the same world of discourse: to see the connexions between Elia and the manufactured televison personality as well as the difference in value between *Lord Jim* and *Captain Condor*. We have to learn confidence in our own real opinions, and this depends on a kind of openness and flexibility, from the beginning, which much academic criticism does nothing to help. It will only ever be real criticism if the process by which judgements are arrived at is shared by all those who are expected to underwrite the judgments or take them over. We can be certain that some of the judgements will not be agreed. But that is all right, for as the argument continues we learn what real criticism is.

Nearly all of us need help in seeing and judging the vast amount of work which comes our way. In education, we must be prepared to look at the bad work as well as the good. The principle in the past has been that once you know the good you can distinguish the bad. In fact this depends on how well you know the good, how well and personally you know why it is good, and how close the bad work is, in form, to anything you have learned to discuss.

I am sure that we are neglecting the world of ordinary communication to which all of us, after education, go home or go on. Yet this has crucial bearings on the whole social process which education is supposed to prepare us for. There are many ways of including this ordinary world. For example:

(i) Regular comparative reading of the range of national newspapers, with a look at headlines and with some detailed comparison of particular stories;

(ii) Discussion of the range of comics, with a detailed look at some kinds of story and drawing, and comparison with relevant stories in books and with stories and essays on similar topics written by pupils. For example, stories about schools in comics could be compared with one or two of the traditional school stories, with contemporary stories such as *Jim Starling*, and with 'before and after' school stories by pupils. As a guide to this, Orwell's essay on 'Boys' Weeklies' might be read and discussed. Or the fairly common 'rebel' stories in comics might be discussed in relation to *Huckleberry Finn*.

(iii) Discussion of advertisements of a particular commodity, alongside one of the *Which?* reports on the same commodity. The commodity could then be used and pupils could write their own reports on it.

(iv) Discussion of selected stories in women's and teenagers' magazines. At a later stage these could be compared, in terms of their implicit values, with the replies to those seeking advice in the same magazines.

(v) A comparative study of 'social images' of particular kinds of profession. For example, compare the version of 'the scientist' or 'the professor' in comics, in science-fiction stories, and in television programmes in which actual scientists appear. Other professions offering relevant material are policemen and detectives (over the whole range from comics and magazines to crime films and plays and documentaries), doctors and nurses, teachers, artists. Varying images of the criminal could also be compared, from a wide range of communications material. The social image of trade unionists could also be looked at, with material from films, television plays, television and radio interviews, and comparative newspaper reports on a particular dispute or strike.

(vi) Comparative visual studies of kinds of modern architecture and design, of the results of town planning and unplanned development, of 'before and after' appearance where an area has been redeveloped.

(vii) Regular discussions of comparable television programmes, e.g., *Z Cars* and *Riviera Police*, *Coronation Street* and *The Newcomers*, *Dr Finlay's Casebook* and *Emergency Ward Ten*.

(viii) Repeat sessions of such programmes as *Juke Box Jury*, both to find ways of discussing pop records critically (this is much more possible than the ordinary cultural attitudes would have us assume), and to compare these with the terms of the televised discussion, e.g., the directive to say whether the record will be a hit, as a question distinct from whether it is liked or thought good, and the use, as pseudo-critical terms, of such adjectives as 'commercial'.

(ix) Writing reviews of a current film, and then comparing

144

them with published reviews, with publicity material, and with recordings of broadcast reviews.

I have done some work along these lines with adult and young-worker groups. I have been very much struck by the way in which, particularly with young workers, ideas for new kinds of study have come from the groups, once the work has been started. Any educational programme of this kind should be sufficiently flexible to allow these new issues to be followed up.

Two general points need emphasis. First, it is unreasonable to ask teachers to do this often difficult work without offering them training in it. The teaching of communications is now sufficiently important to become a regular part of training college work. A good deal of scattered material and experiment is ready to draw on, but needs coordination in relation to training. Two kinds of body are urgently required: a Communications Centre with a staff able to supply catalogues of existing material and to collect and prepare new material, particularly in the expensive visual fields; and an Institute of Communications Research, at university level, undertaking long-range research and analysis (the Centre for Contemporary Cultural Studies at Birmingham is an excellent pioneering example of such an Institute). As these bodies come into existence, links with teachers and with training colleges can easily be arranged. Meanwhile, the supply of facilities to teachers willing to undertake this work, and the support necessary in its early stages, are the responsibility of local education authorities, and it is good to see that several of these authorities are already very willing to assume it.

Second, it is clear that the addition of this work to existing curricula raises many problems of time. But we have to ask ourselves, in view of the importance of modern communications in society, and of their sometimes oblique relation to education itself, not whether we can afford to give the time but whether we can afford not to give it. The work can be done at all stages of education, but it is perhaps particularly important in adolescence: in the leaving years especially, for it is then that the conflict between the values of school and the values of the adult world is most obvious. There is no need, however, for the work to be confined to schools. It should be a central part of the new liberal studies courses in technical colleges, and of apprentice courses. It should form a main part of informal work in the youth service, and it should be a normal subject – it is already increasing – in adult education. We should also remember that a lot of this work can be done through the large communications services themselves: both in general programmes and as part of the now expanding educational programmes. This is particularly important, not only because it can often be done so well in such services as television and radio (though parts of the work will always require the small class), but also because we misconceive the problem if we set education against the major communications systems. There is much in them to criticize, but there is also much to praise. There are many producers already anxious to do this kind of work, both as a part of direct education and because they know how much their own opportunities for doing valuable work depend on the development of an informed, unprejudiced, critical public. In the present very important stage of expansion, it is vital that the many responsible people in communications should work as closely as possible with the educational services, and that teachers and educational administrators (who have often been prejudiced about the newer communication forms, frequently with good if partial reasons) should make a real effort to reciprocate. (See Appendix A.)

AMENDING THE INSTITUTIONS

We cannot leave everything to education and to the most responsible producers. Even if we are not yet ready for fundamental reforms in the institutions of communication, there are many possible amendments within existing social terms. Most people would agree that we want institutions which are both free and responsible. The balance between freedom and responsibility is always difficult to strike, but in many other parts of our social life, and already to a considerable extent in communications, we have agreed on measures to ensure this balance. The proposals now offered are within this tradition.

One clear way of ensuring a balance between freedom and responsibility is to make sure that as many people as possible are free to reply and criticize. Responsibility is then not only a thing we ask other people to maintain. It is what we ourselves exercise, by the right to reply, the right to criticize and compare, and the right to distribute alternatives. All these rights exist in our society, in a general way. Yet many of the institutions of communication are so large and powerful that they can become, in their way, separate empires. Individuals and organizations are free to criticize them, but such criticism can easily be isolated and set aside as unrepresentative or even irresponsible (in fact, for lack of information, it sometimes is irresponsible in the sense that it is wrong). The question is whether we can find ways of ensuring free and responsible comment and criticism, and of distributing the actual range of work.

The Press

The Report of the 1947–9 Royal Commission on the Press recommended the creation of a Press Council, 'to consider where it [the Press] is going and consciously to foster those tendencies which make for integrity and for a sense of responsibility to the public'. It proposed a minimum of twenty-five members, of whom five, including the full-time chairman, should be lay members, eight representing proprietors, four editors, and eight other journalists. Two out of fifteen members of the Commission made reservations that the Press Council should not include lay members. When the Press Council was actually set up, this minority view prevailed, and there were twenty-five members, of whom fifteen were editorial (eight elected by editors' organizations, seven by journalists' organizations), and ten managerial (elected by proprietors' organizations). In 1963, after a further Royal Commission, the Council was reconstituted, to include twenty per cent lay membership, and an independent chairman. The Council meets quarterly, in private, but its General Purposes Committee meets at least monthly. The Council issues special statements and an annual report. Anyone may refer a complaint against a newspaper to the Council, but it is not required to consider complaints by persons not directly concerned with the item, though in practice it has done so. A complaint is first referred to the editor concerned, and is sometimes settled at this stage. Otherwise, the Council considers it, at first through its General Purposes Committee. It invites witnesses, though it cannot compel their attendance, and issues reports and recommendations, though it cannot enforce these. Some editors have complied with recommendations; some have not.

Within its existing terms, the Press Council has done

much good work. It has made many thorough investigations and reports on complaints, and has usefully reminded us that not every complaint against the Press is justified or even accurate. Yet in many fields it is quite without power or even influence (as in the closure of newspapers and magazines, which is one of the most serious current threats to a free Press), and even in its chosen field of specific complaints its authority can be questioned, in view of its composition. It has happened (Muggeridge case, 5th report, pp. 27–8) that an editor complained against has been a member of the Council considering the complaint. It is not stated what procedure is followed in such cases.

In 1961, I wrote that three reforms deserved urgent consideration.

(i) That the majority recommendation on the composition of the Press Council be adopted, thus providing for the inclusion of lay representatives and an independent chairman. The Royal Commission's argument that this would increase the Council's authority, and promote public confidence in it, seems still unanswerable. The degree of direct Press representation would still be such that there could be no question of the Press being controlled by some outside body. Yet the legitimate interests of the rest of society would in this way find some independent voice.

(ii) That while it is obviously wrong that any such Council should have authority over editors, the present position, in which even where a mis-statement of fact has been proved to the Council's satisfaction there is no obligation on editors to correct it, is very unsatisfactory. It cannot be seriously argued that the obligation to correct a publicly proved mis-statement of fact would be a threat to the freedom of the Press in any real sense, and it is clearly in the public interest that such mis-statements should be corrected. The legal position is difficult, but the Council might publicly invite the subscription of all proprietors and editors to this minimum obligation, and publish any such undertakings and refusals.

(iii) That since the major threat to the freedom of the Press is now the fact that newspapers and magazines can be closed down without warning, sometimes overnight, it should be enacted that any such proposal for closure be notified to the Press Council, which would have the duty of inquiring into all the relevant facts, hearing evidence from any persons concerned in the closure (particularly those whose livelihood is directly affected), and publishing its findings. The difficulties here are obvious, but it is even more difficult to take seriously those who say they value freedom of publication, yet claim exemption from timely public inquiry into cases where such freedom is suddenly denied.

Since 1961, some significant progress has been made, in just these fields. The newly constituted Council, under the chairmanship of Lord Devlin, is a more evidently authoritative body, and many of its detailed reports are valuable. The Council has reported that it is now better known to the public, as a resource in cases of complaint. It is possible that, with this increasing authority, the Council will not need to follow the procedures suggested in (ii) above, but vigilance on this important matter is still necessary. The field of changes of ownership, and the problems of concentrated control, remain difficult. The 1962 Commission recommended a Press Amalgamation Court, but the Monopolies and Mergers Act (1965) indicated that questions affecting newspaper ownership and control would be dealt with by a specially appointed panel of the Monopolies Commission, and that this, rather than a court of law, should be the investigating body. The newly constituted Press Council intends to report publicly on changes in ownership and control. If we are thinking of amending rather than changing so important an institution as the Press, it is probable that these lines of development are the right ones: publicity and the machinery of public inquiry are important factors in so public a field. Yet the economic pressures are so great that there is a tendency to leave the matter at the level of report and disquiet. More substantial changes will become inevitable, preferably along the lines discussed in a later section.

Meanwhile, it is worth raising one crucial matter, where Government policy has already a direct influence. The amount of money spent on advertising by Government departments and public undertakings is already a significant factor in press revenue. Some of this advertising is objectionable in itself (see especially the military recruiting campaigns, with their shocking imagery of adventure, and the competing fuel and power campaigns, which make no social or economic sense). But some is useful or marginal (post office, road safety, etc.). At present, the distribution of this advertising, paid for by public money, follows the ordinary commercial patterns, and a newspaper like the *Worker*, for example, has complained of its exclusion. In the eighteenth and early nineteenth centuries, Government advertising was selectively used, for political reasons. Today, the selective pattern is evidently commercial, though given the present social structure of the press it is not without political effect. I believe it is time for a public inquiry into the whole field of Government and public authority advertising, and it would be useful to raise at this inquiry the question of the role of this public money in the present economic structure of the press. A reforming government might well consider whether this flow of public money ought, as a matter of social policy, to be directed in such ways that it counteracts the present alarming development of concentrated press ownership and control. The whole matter is evidently contentious, but the argument should now take place, and in public.

Books and magazines

For the first time ever in Britain we are beginning to get a real range of good cheap books. This may be one of the most important things that has ever happened in our cultural history: that books of a kind which in previous periods would have reached only a very small public can now be easily and cheaply distributed, and in fact find a much larger public. All our old assumptions about 'a tiny minority of serious readers' will have, in practice, to be revised.

Yet the spread of paperbacks, and of cheap educational books of all kinds, is creating new problems. A new kind of owner is coming into publishing, attracted by the new possibility of large profits. The scale of capital involved is rising, and as a direct result there are constant amalgamations of publishers, and the disappearance of many independent houses. Already many of the apparently independent names of publishers, on book jackets, are simply the trading names of different parts of large publishing organizations. This powerful movement towards concentration of ownership is a severe threat to the freedom and diversity of writing. It is not only that fewer people are deciding what ought to be published. It is also that, to succeed in an increasingly competitive market, there is a new emphasis on a reasonably certain and rapid sale. The best publishers are under constant pressure from the competition of the worst, and they get very little public help.

We need to maintain a wide range of independent publishers, and the critical moment is now. As a first step, we need a Books Council, representative of publishers, booksellers, and authors. This Council would collect and publish the existing facts, and would report on all major changes. It would also review existing distribution arrangements, which are near the heart of the matter.

Most towns in Britain are without an adequate independent bookshop. The distribution of books and magazines, outside a few fortunate centres, is in the hands of powerful chains of shops. These chains apply to books and magazines simple tests of quantity. Below a certain likely selling figure, they are not interested, and will not even offer the item for sale. (They are said also to refuse certain publications, on 'moral' grounds. These are not exactly apparent, when one looks at the familiar counters.) Thus the successful book or magazine will get around, but the book or magazine which might be bought, if it were available on anything like equal terms, will in many cases simply not be there. Even in paperbacks, where there is quite good distribution of the full range, there is increasing pressure towards the book that will sell quickly, so that there is no problem of holding stocks. If this situation is allowed to persist and develop, the real opportunities of the coming of cheap books will be missed.

An important part of all new work, in literature and opinion, appears at first in the independent reviews or 'little magazines'. We have a good range of such magazines, of all kinds, but they have little chance with the chain shops. We simply do not know, until we have tried, what public these magazines might actually reach. And the people who say whether we can try or not are the owners of the chain shops.

There is need for a Books Council, simply to publish and review the facts. But I would like to see it go further. It should have the power, and the necessary capital grant, to set up real bookshops in the hundreds of places now served only by the chains. The Council would know, as anyone who uses books and magazines at all closely would know, the difference between a real bookshop and the ordinary chain-shop branch. If it found that in any sizeable community there was no real bookshop, it could either establish its own, or help the public library to establish a bookshop as an ancillary to its lending service, an extension which the development of the reading public now makes reasonable. The chain shops would of course fight this, and might even, in the process, amend their own policies. But if we value the free availability of books and magazines, we should not be afraid of that kind of opposition. The alternative, under existing economic pressures, is an increasingly rigid and mechanical system, under which large publishing organizations feed certain quick-selling items to large distributing organizations, with every kind of minority work restricted to small independent channels. I do not see how anybody who thinks of books as more than simple commodities can stay silent or inactive in the face of that kind of development. But it is not only a matter of expressing opposition. We need an alternative organization, of a positive kind, to unite the many publishers, booksellers, and authors who are already aware of the dangers, and who see the opportunities of the present expansion if it is not allowed to be abused. A Books Council, with generous support from public money as part of our whole educational effort, is now urgently needed.

Advertising

There has been widespread concern, in recent years, about alleged abuses in advertising. In the past, certain safeguards have been codified, notably in relation to the advertising of 'cures' for certain major diseases. Yet a substantial amount of public anxiety remains, and there is a continual but dispersed controversy, between advertising practitioners and their critics, over the facts and values in question. I support the current campaign for a public inquiry into modern advertising (organized by the Advertising Inquiry Committee). In addition to establishing certain badly needed facts (for reassurance or alarm, as the case may be), such an inquiry might consider the institution of an Advertising Council, similar to the Press Council as envisaged by the majority of the Royal Commission. The existence of such a body, to which specific complaints could be referred, by which they would be properly investigated, and with facilities for full and regular public reports, would be a real gain. In addition to investigating specific items, such a Council could sponsor independent research into some of the longer-term issues, such as the effects of certain kinds of advertising, and the difficult question of the relation between the main communication systems and the revenue from advertising on which many of them now depend (with particular attention to the way in which advertising money is now distributed). It will be argued that these matters are best left to the profession itself. But a substantial body of public opinion is not prepared to acquiesce in this, in view of the importance of the issues involved. It is surely time that general public opinion in the matter should be ascertained.

At the time of writing, we are still waiting for the report of the Advertising Commission set up, under Lord Reith's chairmanship, at the invitation of the late Hugh Gaitskell. It remains to be seen whether it has been able to work on the scale of the public inquiry mentioned above; if it has not, the public inquiry should follow. As the years go by, the need for a permanent Advertising Council, similar in composition to the new Press Council, becomes more evident. This is not a matter that can be negotiated by any marginal critique; it is a major issue of social policy.*

Broadcasting and television

The Pilkington Report, published in 1962, marked a major advance in public discussion and awareness of the problems of broadcasting and television policy. The Report was heavily attacked by most of the Press, and there was an evident political nervousness about some of its main recommendations. It remains, however, the classical point of reference for all reform in this field. In particular, its proposal for a further separation of programme provision from advertising, by making ITA rather than the programme companies the advertising contractor, is a sensible first step. Its definitions of a responsible public policy are still the best criteria for judging the performance of the two authorities. In the years since it was published, two main developments can be noted. First, it is clear that the existence of commercial television has radically affected the BBC's attitude to its own services. As could easily have been predicted, the existence of the commercial emphasis, in so central a position, affects the whole field. The BBC, if it is to be responsible, can neither withdraw into a minority position, as most commercial interests would significantly like it to do, nor engage, as it is now increasingly doing, in a competition for audiences on the terms set by the commercial channel. Yet it is bound to follow one or other of these courses, while a major television service designed on the basis of profit rather than use remains in existence. Some signs of more

* The Commission reported while this book was in proof. Its report is in many ways limited and inadequate, but its majority recommendations amount to a useful short-term programme of action and ought, in my view, to be firmly supported.

responsible supervision by ITA, in terms of its original function, and of certain changes of emphasis in the programme companies themselves, can certainly be welcomed, and may indeed be traced to the context of the Pilkington Report. But it is now more than ever certain that we shall have to get rid of a commercial television structure, and especially of this one, with its close connexions in ownership with our already concentrated commercial press. The way forward is the creation of genuinely independent programme companies, which will be leased all necessary production and transmission facilities by an independent public authority. It was perhaps welcome that the BBC got its second channel, but the concentration of control there is also disquieting. If the possible fourth channel is allotted, in a spurious balance, to the existing commercial interests, or to any similar grouping, we shall have lost for a generation any chance of making a genuinely public system. The same can be said of the pressure to give local broadcasting to commercial groups, probably again associated with newspapers. But the alternative is not a limitless extension of the BBC. As each new service comes into technical availability, new forms of organization should be created. We could have, within our existing thinking, four or five independent public corporations, preferably regionally dispersed. (One of these, as noted later, will in any case be necessary if the University of the Air is to be a serious undertaking.) In these ways, it would be possible to start dismantling both the present commercial structure of ITV and the present centralization of BBC, replacing them by a number of public corporations holding production and transmission facilities in trust (with the necessary minimum arrangements for technical coordination), and by a wider range of leasing programme companies, which would be responsible for production policy.

The second fact to be noted, in the years since the Pilkington Report, is the growth of various pressure groups, with an aspiration to affect policy and content. This whole field of representation of the interests of listeners and viewers is extremely difficult. Some years ago it was proposed, notably by the Council for Children's Welfare in its report *Family Viewing*, that there should be a 'Viewers' Council . . . entirely independent of the television authorities and companies . . . a statutory body, not unlike the committee proposed by Sir William Beveridge in his 1949 Report on Broadcasting'. It has also been proposed by the Sound Broadcasting Society that the Council should be enlarged to become a Listeners' and Viewers' Council, and there has been discussion of associating this with the existing Radio and Television Safeguards Committee, which is 'a federation of all the sixteen trade-union and professional bodies operating in the field of radio and television; it covers everybody – actors, technicians . . . and so on'.

These proposals are useful, but everything will depend on the status of any such body. A number of advisory bodies already exist, but it is alleged that they are only rarely consulted on matters of substance. The question is whether it is better to have a completely independent body (with statutory obligation to report), or to work for a Broadcasting and Television Council, similar to those proposed for the Press and for advertising, on which the authorities as well as independent people would be represented. There seem to be clear advantages in the latter, provided there is regular public reporting. It was disquieting to see the brusque rejection, by BBC and ITA, of the recommendations of the O'Conor Committee on Children and

Television Programmes, even where the authorities had themselves set up the committee. A separate monitoring organization would be useful, but a Council in which all issues would have to be publicly argued and reported on is likely to be more in keeping with real public responsibility. It seems to be a fundamental failing of our society that we are continually directed towards a pattern in which on the one hand there are 'the authorities', and on the other hand there are the institutions of opposition and criticism. Each side, we are told, has its part to play. The reality of this usually comes through as an invitation to critics to speak their mind, but then, very often, they are simply brushed off, because 'the authorities', after all, have the final responsibility. I think we shall only get responsible institutions when policies have to be justified in open, equal, and regular discussion, which has a real chance of making some change. A Broadcasting and Television Council might achieve this. A Listeners' and Viewers' Council, while undoubtedly useful, would be important mainly as a step towards a broader sharing of responsibility.

Our continuing difficulty, in finding any open and public solution in this matter, is of course a main reason for the development of the various freelance pressure groups already referred to. I dislike the views of one or two of these groups, but I would insist that arrangements for public criticism and discussion are necessary. Certainly we can all ask who the pressure groups speak for, whether they are really 'the decent people of Britain' or whatever. But we can only ask this question in good faith if we are prepared to envisage genuine facilities for public comment and question. We shall have to see how things go, in the present competition between pressure groups, but it is probable, in my view, that we shall have to come back to the idea of a Broadcasting and Television Council, similar in scope and method to the reformed Press Council, if we are to achieve any settled public balance between freedom and responsibility, and prevent any further development of censorship by authority or demagogy.

Theatre

The Lord Chamberlain now has the power to censor plays. This is so absurd that there ought to be regular demonstrations against it. For it is the survival, in a democratic society, of the purest authoritarianism, made ridiculous by the process of decay. It is sometimes argued that the theatre welcomes this kind of control as an alternative to freedom followed by prosecution. But if guidance is needed, it should not be exercised by the Lord Chamberlain, but by a representative public body (which would also, in the cinema, be better than the present Board of Film Censors, which needs to be brought into the open). It remains arguable whether any such body is really needed. The case for it has to be made out rather than assumed. In other comparable media (particularly on horror and violence in cinema and television) the case has been reasonably made. In the theatre, such a case might be made, but if so it would necessarily be in terms which would show that a Court official cannot meet the need. If we are to be serious about anything, the Lord Chamberlain must go.

General

Any public body can become ingrown or even corrupt, and public responsibility is never fully discharged by the setting up of organizations, however sensibly these are composed. The need for open public discussion and criticism, outside organizations, is absolute. In many ways the conditions for this exist, but there are some important uncertainties. We say we have freedom of comment, within the law, but in practice this is not always how it actually feels. For example, it seems that almost anything can be said about a book or a play or a politician, but that it is dangerous to say the same kind of thing about a soap or a stove or a fountain-pen. It is sometimes said, by editors, that the existing freedom of comment on books and plays depends, legally, on actual invitations to comment on them by sending copies or tickets for review. Whether this is really so in law I am not in a position to say; I have heard it authoritatively doubted. But the effect in practice seems to be of this kind, and I do not think anyone could say that commercial organizations have to face the kind of specific public criticism of their products which is regularly faced by authors and publishers, producers and actors, composers and performers, painters, athletes, politicians, and scholars. The excellent work of the consumers' advisory bodies, in such publications as *Which?*, is now confined to the membership of a particular association, and there are many hints that if it were not so confined it would become subject to 'the law' – a prospect no less menacing because it is vague. Whether this is really so or not, many people learn a practical prudence in this kind of comment. It is right, of course, that we should all be protected from defamation, but the public interest now seems very unevenly defined. Why should not the specific review of products and services be as commonplace in our newspapers and broadcasting and television as the reviewing of books and plays? I wrote in 1961: 'to televise *Which?* would be an invaluable service, and might properly be the BBC's answer to the commercials of ITV'. This is now, in part, being done, in the programme *Choice*, which deserves much more emphasis and a more convenient and popular hour. Some manufacturers argue that they ought not to be exposed to public reports and criticism which might very well, in some cases, turn out to be wrong. What they then have to show, however, is why they should be a special case. So long as there is always the right to reply, open public criticism is central to a good society, and it is surely time to start applying it over the whole range, getting rid of the protected areas. It would be very useful if the law in these matters could be publicly reviewed and clarified, so that we all really know where we stand. Any necessary changes might then also be clarified and worked for.

CHANGING THE INSTITUTIONS

A great deal of good can undoubtedly be done by extending our education in communications and by amending or developing existing institutions. It is certain that this is the work to which we should go as a matter of urgency. Yet it is clear to me that beyond this immediate range certain other actions are necessary. The great majority of those I have called the contributors are employed by groups which have no real responsibility, either to the society or to the cultural purposes they ought to serve. The main feature of such groups is that they provide the capital with which the service can be operated. The society then gets what they decide to offer, and the actual producers are encouraged to compete in supplying it. This seems to me intolerable, in a society wishing to describe itself as free. Yet we are deeply confused in thinking about possible alternatives: partly by the propaganda of the existing groups, who insist very loudly that freedom for them is freedom for everybody; and partly by the genuine difficulties of any public cultural system. We have been reduced to making contrasts between the speculator and the bureaucrat, and wondering which is the blacker devil. The real barrier, perhaps, is that we see these as the only alternatives.

The dangers of State control are real, especially in centralized modern communications. Moreover, our commercial culture emerged by fighting State control, of an earlier kind, and has active memories of its dangers. Against this, many socialists point out that we now have control of another kind, and that it is becoming increasingly centralized. This is true, but until we can show a convincing alternative, which is free of these dangers, it is no kind of reason to change.

I believe that the principle of such an alternative can be stated, and that its practice can be learned. It is this. Where the means of communication can be personally owned, it is the duty of society to guarantee this ownership and to ensure that distribution facilities are adequate, on terms compatible with the original freedom. Where the means of communication cannot be personally owned, because of their expense and size, it is the duty of society to hold these means in trust for the actual contributors, who for all practical purposes will control their use.

Personal ownership is possible in the work of most individual artists. I think much more should be done to provide facilities for such artists, where they are wanted. Local authorities could build studios to let to painters, and bursaries could be offered to young writers and musicians, to go on with their work, just as bursaries are now offered in formal education and scholarship. A good deal of work could be offered to artists, by local education authorities, in the teaching or showing of contemporary arts as described above – particularly, of course, showing (taking this to include readings and performances as well as exhibitions in the visual arts). Artists often teach best by simply showing their work, rather than having to talk about it. Existing experiments such as giving membership of an educational institution to artists, simply to have them there, could be very widely extended. In distribution, there could be many more publicly supported exhibitions and performances, of a local kind. If any artist did not want to use these facilities, he would have the same freedom as now. But we should not assume in advance that all artists prefer to be left alone, when this is understood as left alone to fight through the market, with the constant implication that they would have been all right if they had taken up some 'real' or 'socially useful' job. I am sure that even the most generous offering of facilities of this kind would be met by an even more generous response, from artists glad to show their work and glad to think there are people even potentially interested in it. If funds are needed for these facilities, beyond the ordinary public revenue on which they are already (up to a sixpenny rate) an authorized charge, it would be worth looking at the whole question of the money now made from artists of the past. A ten-year extension of copyright, for example, might be reasonably made the basis of a new trust fund, to be administered by authors' and musicians' professional organizations to help young writers and composers. In the sale of paintings, where large sums of money are now made by speculators and dealers, a compulsory percentage contribution to a similar trust fund could be devised. Such measures would have the advantage of reminding us of the real situation: that while in any one generation artists may need help, and if they get it may find it described as subsidy or charity, in fact, in the history of a people, artists create not only spiritual but material wealth. When this can no longer go to the artists and their immediate families, there is surely no better way of using it than to help their successors, as a matter of right. It is very important to put the question in this way. Everyone seems to ask 'who will pay for the arts?', but what needs to be said – even harshly against some of the ordinary patronage and philistinism – is that the arts pay for themselves, and more than pay. The only real problems are administrative: how to arrange what is in effect the necessary credit, and how to ensure that the values represented by established art are made available to art itself, rather than to private profit or state display.

The proposal for an extension of copyright has now been listed for consideration, in the 1965 White Paper 'A Policy for the Arts'. I hope strongly that it will be followed through. The only objection I have heard is that it is not Treasury practice to earmark income for a particular purpose; this is surely trivial, and could easily be met by one of many administrative devices, or by the creation of an independent Trust to receive the new copyright income. In an open letter, *A Policy for the Writer*, the Society of Young Publishers has supported the idea, and proposed that the period of extension should be twenty-five rather than ten years. The Society goes further and proposes that after the present fifty years, permanent copyright should be vested in the State, to provide money for helping authors. This is a welcome advance, and can be set beside a further proposal of the Society, that we should inquire into the idea of a State publishing house, on the lines of an independent public corporation, with special policies in the reissue of classics and in new noncommercial work. These two ideas – of copyright extension, and a National Publishing House – might eventually be combined, but meanwhile we can work for each on its merits.

At a certain point we touch the edges of that huge cultural organization which is at once the most difficult and the most necessary to reform. In television, in cinemas, in theatres, and in the Press we find a scale of investment beyond the possibility of ownership by individual contributors, and a degree of profit so large as to make any attempt to assert the public interest a fight from the start. I see no alternative, in these fields, but public ownership. The millions of pounds involved could come from no other source. Yet there would be no point in this change if for contributors it was merely the substitution of one form of external control for another. We have to try to combine, in a proper balance, the reasonable provision of public money and the direct freedom of contributors.

We have, fortunately, a precedent, described by Sir Eric Ashby as

a most ingenious British social invention for . . . supervising public expenditure on science and scholarship; the invention of appointing controllers who are drawn from the ranks of the controlled: scientists to administer grants for scientific research, medical men to administer grants for medical research, and academic men to administer grants to universities. It is assumed, and the assumption has been abundantly justified, that controllers of this calibre can determine, better than politicians or administrators can, the criteria for exercising control.

It is true that science and scholarship are different from general communications. But their importance is no greater, to a civilized democratic community. The only alternative to control by a few irresponsible men, who treat our cultural means as simple commodities, is a public system. There will always be tension, in any such system, but the precedent of the universities, which could not survive without public money yet which have retained their academic freedom while accepting it, is important. Theoretically, the State could now dictate to the universities, under the threat of withholding funds. In practice there can be no such dictation, though there can be tension and argument, which in fact are useful. Academic freedom is at least as vulnerable as the general freedom of cultural contribution, yet it has not been killed or weakened by the public system we have. An important element in this, undoubtedly, is that the universities, as bodies, are the organized scholars and teachers to whom this freedom is necessary, and who can defend the principle in a collective way.

Any public ownership of the means of communication should include, as an integral part of its system, the creation of independent professional companies. The outlines of these exist, and much of our best work already comes from companies which can pursue long-term independent policies, creating styles and traditions of their own. Individual journalists, actors, film directors, and producers have usually now to submit to hiring by the financial interests which have real control. Under the new system proposed, the means of communication would be publicly owned but vested in independent trusts which would include representatives of the professions concerned. Use of the media would then be allotted by long-term contract to independent professional companies, which would have full control over content and policy.

In the theatre, for example, some theatres could be nationally owned, some owned by municipalities. In either case a particular theatre (or, to meet real production needs, a group of two or three theatres) would be leased to a company of actors, producers, and dramatists. The main duty of the public trust concerned would be to ensure that the company was adequately organized for the general work it proposed to do, and to see that the range of companies was representative of all trends and schools. Meanwhile it is worth recording that there has been, in the past few years, a marked change of mood, among some local authorities, on this kind of public provision. The best authorities, planning and building theatres and arts centres, are already a model for a generation ahead, and they have received some real encouragement from the proposals in 'A Policy for the Arts'.

In the cinema, film production facilities could similarly be made available to companies of professional film-makers. The cinema circuits could be publicly owned, in two or three networks, and a grant of production facilities would guarantee distribution on one of these. The present concentration of distribution facilities has been referred to the Monopolies Commission, and its report is awaited. But an immediate start could be made on one public circuit, linked to a reconversion of some production facilities to an independent public company. As things now are, film-makers are in the hands of financial controllers who decide whether a film is worth making before it can be made. As Mr Karel Reisz, one of our best young directors, has put it, film makers have to choose subjects 'acceptable to the system', 'not working on the best possible subjects that you want to treat but on the best subjects possible'. In a sensible public system, these decisions would be in the hands of the film-makers themselves, both through the representative public trust and by the giving of contracts for facilities not on the basis of one film but to a professional company aiming to develop its work over several years.

In television, there could be a similar system. The means of production and transmission could be publicly owned but vested in several independent trusts, to include representatives of the actual providers of programmes. The facilities could then be leased, over a period, to professional companies or groups of companies, who would decide their own work. There could be liaison, here, between the professional television companies and the film and theatre companies; also with orchestras and bands, and with the existing guilds of individual contributors.

The BBC has an excellent definition of 'public-service broadcasting', but it exemplifies the dangers of a very large organization, in which producers can become subject to administrators. The development of regional and local broadcasting could become the means of transferring control of this public-service broadcasting to the producers themselves, who already have the nucleus of independent regionally based companies. Here, as in all the proposed companies, it is vital that we should break the pattern of the actual producer controlled by the administrator. There is no reason why all such companies should not be run by ordinary democratic means, with all members having an equal say in discussion of policy, and with administrators working within the definitions of an elected policy, like all other members.

The huge concentration of power in the Press will take a long time to remedy. The first step should be to free local newspapers from remote control by financial empires. A Local Newspapers Trust, in which working editors and journalists would have a majority, could be publicly financed to regain ownership. Local trusts could be organized, to guarantee the independence of editors, with a right of appeal to the national body. A reformed Press Council, retaining a majority of journalists, could then examine the more difficult fields of national newspapers and magazines. The aim should be, as elsewhere, to hold the production facilities in trust, through public ownership where necessary, for allocation to companies of working journalists who would decide their own policies. The functionless financial groups which now control most of our newspapers could be steadily cut out, and the Press restored to the only people capable of guaranteeing its freedom: the working journalists themselves. Meanwhile, the newsprint companies should be taken into separate public ownership. Here is a raw material which should not be tied to particular newspaper proprietors and combines, but should be available, at a fair and open price, to all who wish to use it.

On advertising, there may be some case for particular measures of public safety, along the lines already devised for patent medicines, and there may also be a strong case for reducing the amount of advertising expenditure that is now allowed to be set off against tax. But a more positive answer is very much needed. We need information and advice on the wide range of goods now available, but advertising is a very primitive way of supplying it. A great deal of information about our needs and preferences is now locked up in the offices of advertising agents, who use it only as it suits them, to help them sell a particular product. It is important that this information should be made generally available, if necessary by new independent research, and used in the general public interest as a guide to social and economic policy. The right way to give specific information and advice is that pioneered by the consumers' advice organizations. These should be freed of present legal restrictions, and encouraged, as independent bodies helped by public grant, to extend their work beyond distribution of the kind of printed report which inevitably reaches only a minority. It would be possible to establish actual centres, in the main shopping areas, with the results of tests visually demonstrated, with free advice made available, and with travelling displays and comparative exhibitions of quality and design. Many of the best skills now used in advertising and selling could be used unambiguously for the public good, in such a service. The idea of such centres, first suggested some five years ago, is still hanging fire, but is in many ways stronger than hitherto. An obvious beginning would be two or three pilot centres, in different types of community, for an experimental period.

The communication of real information, and the continual challenge to make judgements of quality, could make a radical difference to our whole economic life, in a proper combination of freedom and responsibility. For it is wrong to set affluence against quality. A central problem of our society is to bring them together, in the common interest. The gimmicks and false appeals which have given affluence a bad name must be challenged in the interests of real use, good design, and a sense of proportion about commodities. Much of the future of our society depends on the growth of real values in this dynamic field. This growth will come about only if we can all take part in it in the course of ordinary living.

CONCLUSION

Many of the measures proposed are radical. All need further definition. But already, at the level of theory, we have broken the deadlock which is so obviously damaging our society. We can conceive a cultural organization in which there could be genuine freedom and variety, protected alike from the bureaucrat and the speculator. Actual work would be in the hands of those who in any case have to do it, and the society as a whole would take on the responsibility of maintaining this freedom, since the freedom of individual contribution is in fact a general interest. At the same time, we would have broken out of the social situation in which it is taken for granted that the arts and learning are minority interests, and that the ordinary use of general communications is to get power or profit from the combination of people's needs and their inexperience. We would be using our means of communication for their most general human purposes.

That is one way of development, but of course it will be opposed. The link with advertising, observed again and again in our study of institutions and methods, is not accidental or marginal. It is the reflection of a society in which commercial interests claim priority in every area of life, and we have had this emphasis and its practical results just long enough to persuade many of us that it is a natural order. The only other effective version of communications in the world is a plain association with the winning or maintenance of political power. Against these versions, with their great institutions absorbing a majority of talent in every generation, we cannot expect any easy struggle. The fact that change will in any case be difficult, that we shall run into many kinds of genuine difficulty and complication, will be tirelessly used to discourage us. There will always be voices, of many kinds, advising us to give up. But in the worst moments, now and in the future, I think we have only to look at the existing situation, clearly and honestly, to recover our energy. The systems have profited so far by each terrifying us with the other, and by the lack of any genuine and attractive alternative. I believe that under pressure the alternative is now emerging, in many minds, and with it a new kind of determination. Any useful change will have to be a genuine discipline, with a real sense of responsibility and with as many people as possible taking part. I think there is a good chance of this happening, but it is only a chance and will need all our strength. At least, now, the challenge is clear.

Further Reading

Some suggestions for further reading and reference are given in relation to the subjects of chapters.

1 DEFINITIONS

Mass Communication by E. Barnouw, Holt, Rinehart & Winston, New York, 1956.

The Bias of Communication by H. A. Innis, Canadian University Paperbacks, Toronto, 1964.

Philosophical Sketches by S. Langer, Johns Hopkins U.P., Baltimore, 1962.

Reader in Public Opinion and Communications by B. Berelson and M. Janowitz, Collier-Macmillan, Glencoe, 1953.

On Human Communication by C. Cherry, Chapman and Hall, London, 1957.

The Nature of Experience by Russell Brain, Oxford University Press, London, 1959.

Mind, Perception and Science by Russell Brain, Blackwell, Oxford, 1951.

Explorations in Communication ed. E. S. Carpenter and Marshall McLuhan, Beacon Press, Boston, 1960.

Vers une Civilisation du Loisir? by Joffre Dumazedier, Editions du Seuil, Paris, 1962.

The Long Revolution by Raymond Williams, Chatto & Windus, London, 1961.

2 HISTORY

The Gutenberg Galaxy by Marshall McLuhan, Routledge and Kegan Paul, London, 1962.

The British Working Class Reader, 1796–1848 by R. K. Webb, Allen & Unwin, London, 1955.

Literature, Popular Culture and Society by Leo Lowenthal, Prentice Hall, New York, 1961.

The Birth of Broadcasting by Asa Briggs, Oxford University Press, London, 1961.

Decline of the Cinema by John Spraos, Allen & Unwin, London, 1962.

The British Film Industry PEP, London, 1958.

The March of Journalism by H. Herd, Allen & Unwin, London, 1952.

The English Common Reader by H. D. Altick, Cambridge University Press, 1957.

Fiction and the Reading Public by Q. D. Leavis, Chatto & Windus, London, 1932.

The Long Revolution by Raymond Williams, Chatto & Windus, London, 1961.

Mass Entertainment; the Origins of a Modern Industry by Asa Briggs, University of Adelaide, 1960.

3 CONTENT

On the Contrary by Mary McCarthy, Heinemann, London, 1962.

Television in Britain PEP, London, 1958.

Facts and Figures about Viewing and Listening BBC, London, 1961.

What Children Watch Granada TV, London, 1960.

Mass Culture ed. B. Rosenberg and D. M. White, Collier-Macmillan, New York, 1958.

The Mechanical Bride by Marshall McLuhan, Vanguard, New York, 1951.

The Popular Arts by Stuart Hall and Paddy Whannel, Hutchinson, London, 1964.

Report of the Departmental Committee on Children and the Cinema HMSO, London, 1950.

Seduction of the Innocent by F. Wertham, Museum Press, London, 1956.

Madison Avenue, USA by M. Mayer, Penguin Books, Harmondsworth, 1961.

The Unholy Trade by Richard Findlater, Gollancz, London, 1952.

Mass Communication by C. R. Wright, Random House, New York, 1959.

The Uses of Literacy by Richard Hoggart, Chatto & Windus, London, 1957.

Culture and Environment by F. R. Leavis and Denys Thompson, Chatto & Windus, London, 1932.

Fiction and the Reading Public by Q. D. Leavis, Chatto & Windus, London, 1932.

Between the Lines by Denys Thompson, Muller, London, 1939.

Dangerous Estate by Francis Williams, Longmans, Green, London, 1957.

Report of the Royal Commission on the Press, 1947–9, HMSO, London.

Performance of the Press PEP, London, 1956.

Broadcasting (Sound and Television) by Mary Crozier, Oxford University Press, London, 1958.

Television and the Child by Hilde T. Himmelweit, A. N. Oppenheim, and Pamela Vince, Oxford University Press, London, 1958.

Family Viewing by Mildred Masheder, Anthea Holme, and Anthony Higgins, Council for Children's Welfare, London, 1960.

Television and the Political Image by J. Trenaman and D. Marsden, Methuen, London, 1961.

Made for the Million, edited by Frederick Laws, Contact, London, 1947.

Voice of Civilization by Denys Thompson, Muller, London, 1943.

The Jazz Scene by Francis Newton, Penguin Books, Harmondsworth, 1961.

Boys Will Be Boys by E. S. Turner, Michael Joseph, London, 1948.

Critical Essays by George Orwell, Secker & Warburg, London, 1946.

4 CONTROVERSY

Report of the Royal Commission on the Press (1961–62), HMSO, London, 1962.

Report of the Committee on Broadcasting (Pilkington Report), HMSO, London, 1962.

British Cinemas and their Audiences by J. P. Mayer, Dennis Dobson, London, 1948.

Against the American Grain by Dwight Macdonald, Gollancz, London, 1963.

Culture for Millions? ed. N. Jacobs, Random House, New York, 1961.

Control or Consent by J. D. Halloran, Sheed & Ward, London, 1963.

The Revolt of the Masses by Ortega y Gasset, Allen & Unwin, London, 1932.

The Advertising We Deserve? by L. Birch, Studio Vista, London, 1962.

Reality in Advertising by Rosser Reeves, MacGibbon & Kee, London, 1961.

The Popular Arts by Stuart Hall and Paddy Whannel, Hutchinson, London, 1964.

Culture and Liturgy by Brian Wicker, Sheed & Ward, London, 1963.

The Immediate Experience by Robert Warshow, Doubleday, New York, 1962.

Techniques of Persuasion by J. A. C. Brown, Penguin Books, Harmondsworth, 1963.

Mass Civilisation and Minority Culture by F. R. Leavis, Minority Press, Cambridge, 1930.

Notes Towards the Definition of Culture by T. S. Eliot, Faber & Faber, London, 1948.

Culture and Society (1780–1950) by Raymond Williams, Chatto & Windus, London, 1958.

Parents, Children, and Television, ITA, HMSO, 1958.

Advertising in a Free Society, Institute of Economic Affairs, London 1959.

The Glittering Coffin by Dennis Potter, Gollancz, London, 1960.

The Nature and Content of Mass Communications by Richard Hoggart, Harvey Memorial Lecture, 1960.

Communication and Community by Raymond Williams, Harvey Memorial Lecture, 1961.

Popular Culture and Personal Responsibility, verbatim report of a conference, National Union of Teachers, London, 1960.

Popular Culture and Personal Responsibility, a study outline, by Brian Groombridge, National Union of Teachers, London, 1961.

The Trial of Lady Chatterley, edited by C. H. Rolph, Penguin Books, Harmondsworth, 1961.

Pressure Group by H. H. Wilson, Secker & Warburg, London, 1961.

The Present Alternatives in Communications by Raymond Williams, Fabian Society, London, 1961.

Socialism and Culture by Richard Wollheim, Fabian Society, London, 1961.

Report of the Commission on Advertising, Labour Party, London, 1966.

5 PROPOSALS

A Policy for the Arts: The First Steps, HMSO, Cmd 2601, 1965.

Film Study Materials, British Film Institute, London.
Youth and the Cinema, British Film Institute, London.
A Handbook of Screen Education, Society for Education in Film and Television, London.
The Teacher Looks at Advertising, National Union of Teachers, London, 1963.
A Policy for the Writer, Society of Young Publishers, London, 1965.
Centre for Audio-Visual and Academic Services, University of Sussex, 1965.
Teaching Film by Grace Greiner, British Film Institute, London, 1955.
Film and Television in Education for Teaching, British Film Institute, London, 1959.
English for Maturity by David Holbrook, Cambridge University Press, 1961.
Popular Culture and Personal Responsibility, National Union of Teachers, London, 1960.
Possibilities for Local Radio by Rachel Powell, Centre for Contemporary Cultural Studies, Birmingham, 1966.

PERIODICALS

The Use of English, Chatto & Windus, London.
New Left Review, London.
Athene, Society for Education through Art, London.
Contrast, British Film Institute, London.
Sight and Sound, British Film Institute, London.
Which?, The Consumers Association, London.
Slant, Sheed and Ward, London.
Views, London.

Appendix A:
Methods in TV Education

A marked and welcome change in the uses of television in recent years has been the development of educational programmes. A sample in November 1965 showed the following hours and kinds on the two main channels.

November 1965	Hobbies	Languages	Other General Education	Schools and Technical Colleges
BBC I	2.00	1.30	2.20	14.30
ITV (Anglia)	—	0.20	0.20	5.31

The BBC was doing almost all the adult and general educational programmes, and had also a much more extensive provision of special courses for schools, technical colleges and other branches of further education. It should be noted that schools programmes are repeated at least once, sometimes twice or more. Because of the importance of this work, it is important to give some independent assessment of its methods and quality. The following comments are based on extended observation of all kinds of programme.

In certain fields, the discovery of new educational techniques, or the use of television to reinforce existing techniques, has fully justified work that must still be regarded as in an experimental stage. The language programmes deserve special mention. These, on BBC especially, have united some of the methods of the language laboratory, involving prepared and phased participation by the student, with forms copied from televised drama, in which short scenes, with continuing and named characters, are acted by native speakers of the language concerned, and used as a basis for the subsequent teaching. The courses are supplemented by booklets and records, and their only weakness, in what is as a whole a fine achievement, is the lack of any planned connection with further work and study. The language programmes for schools on ITV – in French only – are evidently planned for use in collaboration with normal teaching: the illustrated talks are wholly in French, and there is no direct teaching by television; rather a provision of useful listening practice. These have been well and imaginatively presented.

The BBC programmes, both schools and general, on science and allied subjects have also been well done. In the general courses, the characteristic method is an illustrated lecture course, by university scientists. The opportunities for detailed visualization and illustration have on the whole been well taken. Once again the weakness is the lack of connection with further work and study, and the attempt to stage participation, by having the lectures given before audiences, who in some cases have been encouraged to ask what sound like prearranged questions, has been unsuccessful. These defects are only likely to be overcome when such programmes are part of a television education service planned as a whole, and with specific links to both normal and specially devised educational institutions. What the experiment has so far shown is that reasonably advanced lectures are both possible and interesting on television, and can be used as a method in the next stage of organic development. In the schools courses, the link to further study already exists, and the programmes in science, mathematics and (often outstandingly) in geography have been well done.

It is necessary to make a clear distinction between the programmes already discussed, in which a body of impersonal knowledge is imaginatively presented, and a whole range of programmes, involving immediate judgement, controversy and personal selection, which turn out, on examination, to be very much less satisfactory. In a sense, of course, it is inevitable that this should be so, but some of the divergences noted have been so striking, and this field is in any case so important, that some detailed scrutiny is necessary.

An initial example may be taken from schools drama programmes. The range of plays chosen has been excellent, and some of the productions have been good. But there has been a marked reluctance to let the plays speak for themselves, or, when commentary has been supposed to be necessary, to provide either factual introduction or critical commentary. Instead, there is often a kind of introduction which positively defeats the purpose of the productions. One example is the linking of *Sergeant Musgrave's Dance* and *The Good Soldier Schweik*, at the casual level of reactions to war, and without any attempt to provide a critical frame of reference. This is wholly unacceptable. The plays mentioned were presented as if they were, in effect, documentaries, and interest was led away from their specific methods. The combination of a kind of visual sophistication and an essential ignorance was very disturbing, and it was a positive relief when the so-called introduction stopped and there was a chance to look at the play. The difference in level between this and the talks, in French, on twentieth-century French writers, in the language programmes, was very striking, and yet the latter could hardly have been said to be the easier operation.

There is a range of programmes of a general knowledge kind which vary markedly in quality. The BBC's *Spotlight* is usually good; its *Signpost* is much more variable. ITV's *Afternoon Edition* is an interesting example of the combination of advanced technique with virtually worthless material. A journalist speaks on some topic in current affairs, and then answers questions phoned in by children at schools. It is not only that the questions are usually very inadequately answered, but that the false excitement of the telephone calls arriving seems to have been accepted as an adequate substitute for any serious attempt to follow the questions and misunderstandings through. It is doubtful if such work is educational at all. The absence of social studies from most of our schools is indeed shocking, but this kind of programme – characteristically oriented to the hurried world of newspapers, and with the sense of hurry presented as a value in itself – is essentially a way of assimilating children to the adult world without giving them any properly informed guidance to understanding it. A similar kind of assimilation, though one using very different techniques, is the BBC programme *Going to Work*. This might be thought to involve an informed introduction to different kinds of adult work, with some attempt to relate specific jobs to the range and character of work as a whole, in our kind of society. Instead it amounts, often offensively, to a course in 'what your employer will expect of you', the details of the work being subordinated to this kind of training in adjustment. This seems to me, under its harmless guise, to be simple indoctrination, of a kind similar to the so-called advice on careers in the magazines for adolescent girls.

When social issues are a matter of history, they can be handled very well in television education. Some of the best programmes seen were in the ITV series *The Railway Age* and *The Land and the People*. Such work represents a fine accession to our educational resources. But when it is a question of contemporary social issues, it is a very different matter. I want to look in some detail at two educational programmes on advertising, the first in the ITV series *English and Life*, and the second in the BBC series *Living in the Present*. I ought to say that I have a particular interest in the latter series, since in the programmes on communications some of the methods and material were comparable with parts of the first edition of the present book, though it is worth adding that neither *Communications*, nor *Culture and Society* and *The Long Revolution*, which are on most booklists of this kind, appeared in the list of forty-seven items in the booklet for lecturers ('The books in this list have been selected for several reasons. Some are directly relevant to our programmes, while others will be of use to students who wish to follow up for themselves the various subjects we shall be introducing. The majority are readily available, many in paper-back form.').

The ITV programme was amateurish. The main technique of its first part was a mock-angry argument between two actors, representing an industrialist and a communist, who exchanged routine cliches about their systems, with advertising as the peg. There followed an extraordinarily rapid illustrated survey of the history of human industry and production, from an African village to the present. Some examples of contemporary advertising were then introduced, from the field of public advertising in such matters as road safety. The children were then advised to collect examples of advertising for themselves.

It is fair to say that this never sounded like education. The raising of vague general questions, and a generalized invitation to participation, seemed useless in the confused and confusing context of the material actually presented. The mock argument is perhaps the key, because it appeared to satisfy the need for discussion, in a matter bound to be controversial, yet succeeded in reducing it to a kind of variety sketch. The odd bad programme must always be expected, but there seems to be something more at work here: the issues are about, and must be discussed, but a particular tone can be set, the more effectively if the superficial effect is one of amateurism. The industrialist was not attractively presented – he had a double chin, and was given coarse arguments – but it also stays in the mind that the critic of advertising was a wild young communist, quoting foreign experience. Meanwhile the laughable version of the history of human economy provoked the most serious comparison with the brilliant social and economic history programmes already referred to.

The BBC programme on advertising was much more professional in appearance. It began with a speaker addressing a women's group in Brighton. She said that advertisers often claim a lot for their products. 'Soap will make us beautiful as well as clean' (laughter). The programme then moved to an interview with a representative of the Institute of Practitioners in Advertising. Whereas the first speaker had been overheard, this man spoke directly to camera, in reply to questions from an interviewer. It is worth noting that the interviewer was polite and respectful, and accepted the speaker's replies without question. The general line of these replies was that advertising increased sales, and that this was its main recommendation. He saw no reason why advertising of cigarettes should be banned, since cigarettes were on sale in the shops. No attempt was made to connect the implications of these answers. The representative smoked while replying. He was sitting in an impressive office. The programme then moved to an interview with a representative of a detergent manufacturer, who described a packet which contained 18 per cent more of the product than those at a comparable price: this had been marketed in response to criticism of selling detergents with gimmicks, but was not preferred by housewives to packets with less of the product but with a 'present' attached. No comment was made by the interviewer. The programme returned to the woman speaker ending her talk to the group. A voice asked us, in conclusion, who we agreed with.

The method, here, requires very careful study. The programme could be justified as presenting 'both sides' of the argument, but the distribution of emphasis, and the ways in which the different speakers were seen and allowed to speak, add up to a very different reality. Thus no evidence was taken on the economic arguments about advertising, except the apparently authoritative statements of an advertising agent. The detergent example, which could have been followed up by questions about the percentage of advertising costs in detergent prices, was left as it stood, though it was only marginally an example of *advertising* at all, and this marginal element – the relative failure of a campaign to get people to buy the packet with 18 per cent more of the product – received no discussion or even emphasis. In its more professional way, this programme, like the ITV programme, set an influential tone and approach. 'Critics of advertising' were generalized, though in one aspect of the case overheard; the spokesman for advertising was from the inside, giving unchallenged opinions. The voice asking whom we agreed with might be taken as the impartial voice of education, but in its actual context, and with no other information available, it was in effect rhetorical. My final impression of this programme was that, although presented as education, it followed closely the techniques of a particular kind of public relations, itself closely related to a familiar form of 'defensive' advertising. Some criticism is admitted, but in its least powerful and least specific form. This has the effect of suggesting a fair-minded approach. But then the real content is presented, straight to camera and with the supporting images of authority. (Students of this technique can be referred to the edited *Gallery* version of the 1965 Oxford teach-in on Vietnam, in comparison with the direct sound broadcast, taking the course of the argument as it came, on the Third Programme.)

I find it very disturbing that such work can be transmitted as education by a public authority. That such programmes can be properly prepared needs no argument; an example is to hand in the programme on television and cinema in the same series, where a variety of professional evidence was taken and discussed. A programme on the Press, on the other hand, reverted to the 'insider' approach: it showed the process of launching the *Sun*, and then presented certain critical points – on the Press Council, the effects of advertising on policy, concentration of ownership, and sensationalism – which were all answered by Lord Francis-Williams: not indeed as blandly as in the case of the points about advertising, but wholly within the habits of thought of practitioners in the institution under discussion.

It is of course to be expected that education involving contemporary values and social policies raises difficulties not present in education in languages or in reasonably settled bodies of scientific knowledge. But it has to be said, on the evidence of the programmes watched, that the contrast in standards of professionalism and responsibility, between these two kinds of work, is shocking and intolerable. One is forced to remember that whereas in language and science the immediate producers of these programmes have no claim to competence, and so turn to the universities and similar institutions, in the case of drama, and in the world of current affairs and communications, they are themselves often practitioners, belonging in varying degrees to the world on which they are supposed to bring an educated mind to bear. It seems essential, if television education is to expand to the extent and at the standards which are necessary, that the responsibility for programmes should be made unambiguously educational, through an independent body composed of people who have primary educational loyalties, and who can in the course of experiment arrive at working standards of the kind achieved in normal educational institutions. TV-education producers and writers, that is to say, should be administrators and teachers within a primarily educational body, with close links to all those working in traditional education, rather than a separate group of 'communicators', working in another kind of world, and all too often, at the revealing crucial points, drawing their habits and standards from such a world rather than from education itself. Meanwhile it is much to be hoped that teachers and pupils will find time and ways to inspect, critically, the methods of television education itself, as well as the matters to which their attention is formally and often powerfully directed. On the evidence of what I have seen, and with much excellent work to form an immediate point of comparison, this kind of critical examination is necessary and even urgent.

It might be worth mentioning, finally, the project for a University of the Air. The case for a specific educational channel – in fact the fourth channel – is very strong, and there is enough early evidence to show that a properly integrated service, with links to correspondence and other follow-up courses, could be provided. But if it is, it must be, in its essential character, a university: that is to say, it must be a primarily academic and teaching body, with some permanent academic staff as well as the services of teachers from other institutions, and with its producers and technical staff as specialist members within an educational body. There are still many difficulties (not least of finding enough time for all that might be done), but so striking a development could be our most important cultural advance for a generation.

Appendix B:
A Policy for the Arts

COMMENTS ON THE 1965 WHITE PAPER
(reprinted from the author's article in *Tribune*, 5 March, 1965)

From the October campaign to the February white papers is a long season. This hard grey light of late winter is as cold as stone, and the country looks bare, because there is not enough growth to absorb the lengthening days. In such a landscape, Jennie Lee's white paper – a policy for the arts – is like the first snowdrop: a flower certainly, but small, isolated, the colour of the season.

'We walk the same streets, breathe the same air, are exposed to the same sights and sounds.' That is the root of the policy she is arguing: a sense of community, and of the arts as its breath of life, but tinged, in its very language, with a sense of restlessness and exposure. 'A new social as well as artistic climate is essential.' We are not likely to doubt that. 'A Policy for the Arts: the first steps': promise and limitation, in the same phrase.

'We have been in the habit of financing some fields of the arts on no more than a poor law relief basis. . . . All new social services have to fight long and hard before they establish themselves. Only yesterday it was the fight for a free health service. The day before it was the struggle to win education for all.' This, clearly, is Jennie Lee's own perspective, and of course it is right. Behind the words is the memory of Aneurin Bevan, and the sense of the Labour movement so many of us shared with him. And just because this is so, she will not lack allies, but she will need them, badly.

The best single thing, in these new proposals, is the transfer of Government responsibility for the arts from the Treasury to the Ministry of Education. This is not just administration; it is, or ought to be, policy. Jennie Lee's temporary home, at the Ministry of Public Building and Works, was obviously wrong: art as prestige and preservation. Treasury control is equally wrong: art as a minor object of patronage and subvention. Any real policy for the arts is an educative policy: part of a whole growth of mind and activity. I did not expect this transfer of emphasis to happen so soon. The energy we had reserved, to campaign for it, must go now into securing it. Just as a token: alter the brass plates and the notepaper to Ministry of Education, Arts and Science. For a few years, until we get a Ministry of Arts. After all, we are moving. '*Leisure for Living*' still had a nervous tic about 'state nannies': frightened in its cradle by the *Daily Express*. But the White Paper can say: 'certain sections of the Press, by constantly sniping at cultural expenditure, made philistinism appear patriotic'. It is still a long way to go, but we are starting to use our own voices.

These changes of basic policy, of a long-term kind, matter more than the immediate sums of money. The Arts Council grant goes up from £2,150,000 to £2,815,000. The grant for museums from £54,000 to £108,000. A primer fund, for capital spending on housing the arts, is started at £250,000. Within the Arts Council grant, the fund for helping individual artists goes up from £10,000 to £50,000. All these increases are welcome. All, of course, are too small. But we do not want, as a first priority, simply to send more money along the existing channels. We want to broaden and alter the channels, and make new ones. The White Paper agrees, in general terms. That must be the meaning of replacing 'poor law relief' with 'a new social service'. In particular terms, though, it is still vague.

There will have to be a fight, quite soon, about the Arts Council. Within its limits, it does good and necessary work, but the limits are obvious. 'To increase the accessibility of the fine arts to the public throughout Our Realm': what policies, what men, do you get, from a definition like that? Accessibility; fine arts; the public: these are the words of paternalism, and in matters of art the English upper-middle class are in any case improbable fathers. The same with Regional Associations, which the White Paper recommends. Are they to go the way of Regional Gas Consumers Advisory Councils? You live in a region, and one day on a list in the Post Office you see a lot of names and decorations which are notionally you and your neighbours. I would prefer to talk about real places: cities and towns and counties; the arts centres you can build in them; the region as a working, co-ordinating arrangement; very practical, too busy for leisured people to get to; no honours in it, no patronage, no receptions; a working office. All the way through, and ultimately changing the Arts Council, we want this hard democratic system: power where the work is being done, and the regional and national boards and committees as places of working co-ordination, not advice and patronage.

The White Paper can be read both ways. Part of it proposes, or seems to propose, the white paper bodies we do not want, and approves the white paper bodies we already have. Part of it, on the other hand, is about real places and people. The capital building fund is a challenge to local authorities to start building: as the need rises, the fund will rise. If this is bluff, we must call it, in every local authority area. And if this kind of growth, already active in some places, is really coming, then we shall have the basis for radically reforming the present national administration, the Boards of Guardians who will have been outgrown.

Meanwhile, some local clearing up. The White Paper proposes planning control on any change of use in theatres, other than to a cinema or music-hall. That is necessary. It discusses new ways of raising the money to help living artists: state money, a levy, an extension of copyright. I hope the last is accepted, and the fund extended to all the arts. And the sixpenny rate provision to apply to counties: that would be good. In the next White Paper, the Lord Chamberlain can be retired.

Local reforms and radical reform: any Labour Government, obviously, must be committed to both. It is worth looking ahead, with the White Paper in mind. I was struck by one paragraph:

'. . . diffusion of culture is now so much a part of life that there is no precise point at which it stops. Advertisements, buildings, books, motor cars, radio and television, magazines, records, all can carry a cultural aspect and affect our lives for good or ill as a species of "amenity".'

But we must get this right. 'Carry a cultural aspect': do we need a redraft or a rethink? Does it mean advertisements could be more 'cultural'? Like the earlier sentence which distinguishes 'light entertainment' from 'cultural projects'? I think it does, and if so we have to be rough with it. But the other words could mean something important: that culture isn't just the 'fine arts', as opposed to the 'coarse arts' presumably; that cultural values refer to our whole living, and not to a grace note in the margin. I have marked about twenty places in the White Paper, where this fundamental *choice* is blurred; the phrases can lead either way. In the long run, this issue is crucial. The 'younger generation', referred to on the first page, are not 'more hopeful material': they are nobody's damned material at all. We are talking about a society, not about processing.

But if we are talking about a society, Jennie Lee will soon have to say that her brief is too narrow. For the major cultural fact, about Britain, is the extreme monopoly in all kinds of communications. The narrowness of our art is a social symptom directly parallel with this. We shall not change one without changing the other, and we shall not change either without radically changing the society.

In fact the White Paper refers to the monopoly in film distribution: it has been referred to the Monopoly Commission. All right, we will watch it through. It touches on radio and television, but a bit piously, along the line that Government mustn't interfere. As if the whole structure of sound and vision broadcasting in Britain were not a political act, subject to political change. And anyway, I suppose, nervous about treading on another department: the Post Office of all places. The next administrative reorganization might recognize the fact that television and radio aren't like letters and telephones, but are cultural institutions. The necessary links between artists and companies, in different parts of the country, and our major national and regional performance network, on sound and television, depend on this problem being seen and treated as a whole. But then to see radio and television in this way, serving these varied national and regional and local purposes, means challenging the existing structure, which has got profit and the State built into it, and of course, as in all mixed economies, becoming more

like each other. It will take time, but there will be no real
policy for the arts, no serious linking of cultural and
educational policies, until we have looked again at our
majority services.

Of course nobody dares, from Whitehall, even to look
at the Press, for all its rampant monopoly. That will not
cease to be philistine merely by changing its local policy
on spending on the fine arts; it has all the rest of life to
be philistine about. Could we not begin in at least some
areas: magazines, for example? But there is in any case a
more immediate and tractable area: the present
condition of publishing and bookselling. Who deals
with that? The Board of Trade? Whoever it is, it needs
looking at, for it is directly affecting literature. It will be
a long and complicated business, but that is why we
need a public inquiry started now.

And again, advertising. There is the biggest employer of what might be the skills of some real art. Its
command of money exerts its pressure into almost every
field of art and communication. I repeat the existing
challenge. If we are serious about art and communication, and if we are serious about production for use
and not for profit, we must start thinking about positive
changes, as well as the local controls already being
canvassed and enacted. Let us have, beside the Arts
Centres, the design or service Centres, in which
independent information about goods and services is
freely and attractively presented: the basis of a real
education, in which we learn from each other about real
use and real design, and get some standards by which
we can judge our economy. Put this kind of work beside
the galleries and the concert halls and the theatres and
the libraries and the bookshops, and we can then be
serious about culture.

'A Policy for the Arts: the first steps.' First steps, it is promised, towards 'a fully comprehensive policy'. Jennie Lee and her colleagues need all our support, if the promise is to be kept. But support from where we are, and from how we see the problems. We don't, most of us, travel up to London, to hear the Minister's point of view. And this Minister, I hope, wouldn't want us to. It is our business, in our work, to have our own points of view, and to keep the argument public. Now that the first snowdrop is out, we will help, of course, to see it isn't trampled on. We will say how much we like it, so small, so isolated, in its colours of the season. And we will look for the other flowers that we are entitled to expect will follow it, after so hard and long a preparation of the ground.

Postscript (May, 1966)

That was one way – and still, so far as Jennie Lee is concerned, a relevant way – of responding to the Labour Government's policies in these fields. But I have since read Harold Wilson's speech at the Guildhall dinner on the tenth anniversary of ITV (*ITA Notes*, October 1965). I will say only that it affected me like the dinner at the end of George Orwell's *Animal Farm*. It should perhaps be added that some of the proposals on broadcasting and television emerging from Mr Wilson's government, through that curious channel, the Postmaster-General's department, are unbelievably bad, and need to be fought without respect to anniversaries or governments.